D1506094

Introduction by Frank Gehry

# EXPERIMENTAL ARCHITECTURE IN LOS ANGELES

Essays by Aaron Betsky, John Chase, and Leon Whiteson

Los Angeles Forum for Architecture and Urban Design

*RIZZOLI*
NEW YORK

Front Cover:

Central Office of Architecture

**"SiteWorks: Investigations of the Inbetween"**

UCLA Graduate School

of Architecture and Urban Design Gallery

Los Angeles, CA 1990.

Frontispiece:

Hubert/Zelnio with Gealle Breton and David Leclerc

**"SiteWorks: Investigations of the Inbetween"**

UCLA Graduate School of Architecture and Urban Design Gallery

Los Angeles, CA 1990.

Panoramic photographs of Los Angeles (pp. 6–7, 42–43, 82–83, 130–131)

by David Rosten

Back cover illustration (hardback only):

Schweitzer BIM,

**The Monument**

Joshua Tree, California  1987–90

First published in the United States of America

in 1991 by Rizzoli International Publications, Inc.

300 Park Avenue South, New York, NY 10010

Library of Congress Cataloging-in-Publication Data

Experimental Architecture in Los Angeles/introduction by Frank Gehry:

essays by Aaron Betsky, Leon Whiteson, and John Chase.

p. cm.

ISBN 0-8478-1424-6 (HC)

ISBN 0-8478-1338-X (PBK)

1. Architecture, Modern-20th century California Los Angeles.

2. Avant-garde (Aesthetica) California Los Angeles History 20th century.

3. Architecture California Los Angeles.

4. Los Angeles. II. Chase, John 1953-  III. Whiteson, Leon.

NA735.L55E97  1991                90-23643

720'. 97949409045-dc20                CIP

Designed by Lorraine Wild and Lisa Nugent / ReVerb, Los Angeles

Printed in Singapore

**ACKNOWLEDGEMENTS**

8

This book documents a series of discussions organized by the Los Angeles Forum for Architecture and Urban Design at the Schindler House and the Substation for Architecture in Los Angeles in 1988 and 1989. Entitled "Out There Doing It," this series offered young practitioners the chance to discuss their work with their peers. The Los Angeles Forum for Architecture and Urban Design is a non-profit group that offers a forum for the discussion of architectural issues through lectures, publications and special events.

The series was organized by John Kaliski, Kris Miller and Aaron Betsky, with help from the members of the Forum. The material for this book was collected and edited by Aaron Betsky, John Chase and Leon Whiteson. Invaluable assistance in editing was provided by David Morton and Dan Waterman of Rizzoli International Publications, and by Natalie Shivers. The book was designed by Lorraine Wild with Lisa Nugent, who together helped give coherent shape to the mass of material. The Forum would also like to thank Ann Zollinger, Robert Sweeney, Peter C. Haberkorn and all the members of the Forum who helped make this book possible.

# L E T A THOUSAND

By Frank Gehry

# FLOWERS B L O O M

When I began to find my style there simply wasn't much of a support system for anyone trying to do something different. There weren't a lot of people I could talk to. The established firms jealously guarded their turf and considered the few of us who were trying to innovate as interlopers who threatened their sense of security.

The man who did the most to change this mean situation nationally was Philip Johnson. He gave architecture a high public profile, upped the dialogue and the exposure and, by his own example, urged practitioners to encourage innovation and pass on work to unusual talents. His generosity was very compelling, and certainly helped keep me going through disheartening times. It was an important model.

At the time, too, when Moss and Morphosis were just starting out, we were fortunate to have a sympathetic voice in the media in John Dreyfuss, at *The Los Angeles Times*. Dreyfuss, the journalist son of Henry Dreyfuss, wrote profiles of people like Thom Mayne and Eric Moss, and helped them get work. Since he stopped covering architecture there's been a big hole in media coverage of the younger guys.

Designers were kind of isolated in my day, and I found my community among artists rather than architects. Nowadays there's more of a sense of an architectural community here. I'm not as much a part of that community as I would like, and I don't have nearly enough contact with these kids. I guess I'm still struggling with my own insecurities, despite all the recent publicity and recognition my work has had. Every time I grapple with a design problem I feel as vulnerable as I ever did, and that makes me self-centered, like most creators.

Teaching is one way to maintain contact with the younger generation, and I taught a studio at UCLA last year, and have taught at SCI-ARC, Yale, and Harvard. But now I'm just too busy. I hardly even have time for my family.

Yet, generally, there's more of a support system today. I recommend young designers whenever I can, in the Johnsonian spirit. And there's certainly a wider public acceptance of avant-garde architecture in L.A. Given this, I keep urging the kids not to become disillusioned or cynical about the scene.

If I was any kind of model, it was in showing that you could take small commissions and make something of them. You don't have to get the big stuff to make your mark. And maybe we've created a climate of risk-taking, have created a constituency for the new that encourages younger clients to go with interesting talents. And I pass on work. In fact, it often happens that clients ask me to recommend someone young for a job I'd like to do myself! I only hope Frank Israel, Moss, and Morphosis are also passing opportunities along.

Looking over the array of work presented in this book, I see some I think is wonderful, other stuff that seems trivial. But that doesn't matter, and it's not really up to me to play judge and jury. Some of these guys I know well, like Paul Lubowicki, who worked with me for a long time. I understand how he's struggling to find his own agenda.

I truly don't see that I've directly influenced any of these kids. I have my own strict set of rules in my head, and I don't recognize any of my ideas in the work of people like David Kellen, Josh Schweitzer, or Koning Eizenberg. They just haven't followed my rules, so far as I can see. Maybe they've copied my mannerisms rather than my method, but I see them following very independent ideas of their own. For example, the little house Koning Eizenberg did near my own uses a kind of green tone that seems closer to what Arata Isozaki did at the Museum of Contemporary Art downtown than to anything I might do.

Have I spawned a school, as some people claim? I don't see it, and I certainly don't want the responsibility. But I am excited by the sheer energy these kids display. Time will sort out the few real talents from the general run, and define the nature of their collective style.

Looking at the change in the Los Angeles context from the 1960s and 1970s to the 1990s, I have to say that things are more sophisticated, but they're also more threatening and more desperate.

One of the biggest changes is that people here are beginning to accept the fact that this is a city, a very particular metropolis, not a makeshift collection of communities. A lack of acceptance of Los Angeles's reality hampered me a lot twenty years ago; it delayed acceptance of my kind of work, which went along with the grain of the place rather than attempting to ignore it, or pretend it should be like New York.

But I'm troubled by the disturbing impulse among the establishment to rebuild Rome, to create a polite, almost classical order the people in power feel is the mark of a true city. This wrong-headed impulse has made us miss several fundamental opportunities, such as the chance to build upon the kind of Wilshire Boulevard-type linear downtown Los Angeles pioneered in the 1930s. Instead, we've created, in central L.A., a belated and mediocre copy of Manhattan or Dallas that has helped foul up our transportation system.

In L.A. I've long been considered strange and odd, a "maverick." For years, no big corporation or major developer gave me a commission of any size. Disney Hall, which I won in close competition with Stirling, Hollein, and Boehm, is the first big thing I've been given to do in my home town.

In Los Angeles, despite all its freedom to experiment, the avant-garde remains peripheral to the mainstream of most of what's being built. This means that young designers have to choose between being subsumed into the system, or surviving on such crumbs as garage remodeling. I managed by working in both camps, and when the system got too much in my way, I backed off and disappeared into my own life.

Now some of these young guys come out of school and straightaway start doing it — and a lot of the work looks not quite cooked. The quality of imagination and accomplishment is pretty uneven. But a lot of the things older architects are doing also look half-baked. Time will sort out the wheat from the chaff. One or two talents will become real heavyweights. The others contribute to a level of excitement that's creating a lasting constituency for good design in this town.

One thing we desperately need here is a showcase for architecture, like Mickey Friedman established at the Walker Art Center in Minneapolis. No other museum in the world has given innovative designers the exposure the Walker has. We're trying to create something like that here, so far with little success.

There is still a lot of creative opportunity here. When I visit New York, Chicago, or Milan, for instance, the young architects do a lot of talking but have few chances to build anything. The opportunity exists in L.A. because of all the craziness of Hollywood, the ambiance of innovation generated by high-tech industries such as aerospace and electronics, and of course the benign climate that allows a lot of ricky-ticky construction that wouldn't survive long in harsher latitudes. Maybe Miami, with a comparable climate, a similarly diverse ethnic mix, and a feeling of creative freedom as the southland, has a chance to foster such diversity and experimentation.

Of course, in today's context of homelessness, for example, many people say experimental design is a trivial pursuit. But I don't see it that way. I think that artistic expression is the juice that fuels our collective souls, that innovation and responding to desperate social needs are not exclusive imperatives.

We've got to think of ourselves as generating something worthwhile, something that's alive at all levels. This garden of young talent represented here is one that's very worth watering.

# AKS RUNO

**BARHAM SHIRDEL**

Education:

Bachelor of Architecture
University of Toronto, 1979
Master of Architecture
Cranbrook Academy of Art, 1982

**ANDREW ZAGO**

Education:

Bachelor of Fine Arts
University of Michigan, 1980
Master of Architecture
Harvard University, 1986

**Olympic West Office Towers Competition** West Los Angeles, California 1988

A competition for the design of two office buildings and the urban design of the major east-west thoroughfare that separates their two sites gave rise to this entry. The design attempts to create two distinct public spaces; the split nature of the program was used to challenge the traditional notions of monumentality in the city.

13

14

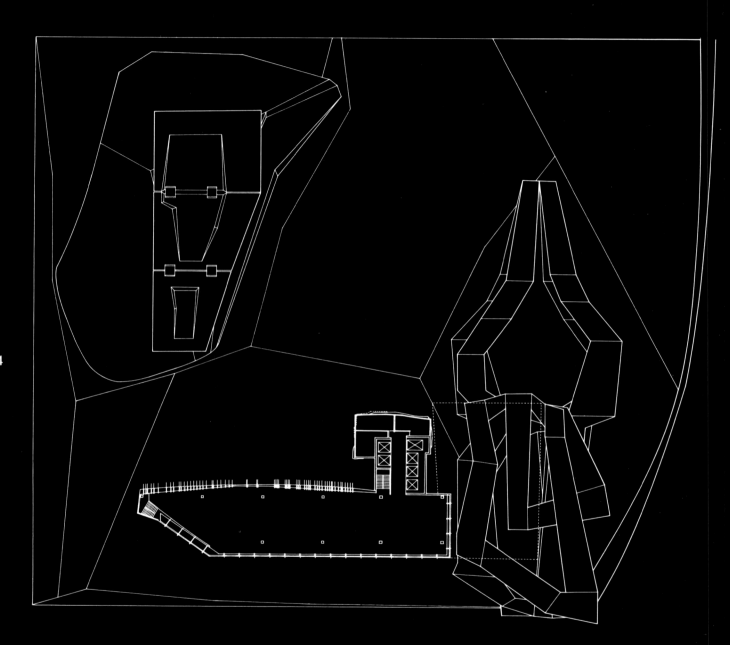

Plan at base

16

**Alexandria Library** Alexandria, Egypt 1989

This competition entry for a public library in Alexandria, Egypt, employs an organic vocabulary, its forms suggestive of ocean waves. Elements of the design include a stack plinth, an anteroom, a reception space, and a veil which extends the library beyond its site boundaries. The building is meant to pay tribute to the spirit of invention housed in the ancient library of Alexandria and to recall the forms of the nearby sea.

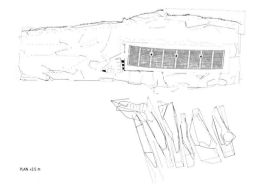

PLAN +3.5 m

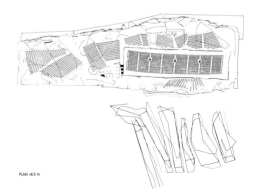

PLAN +6.5 m

Plans

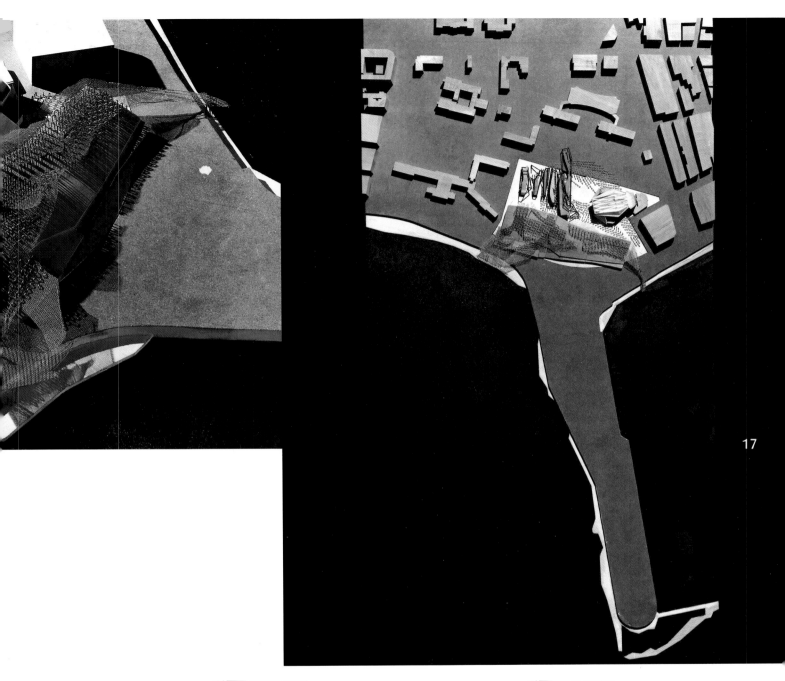

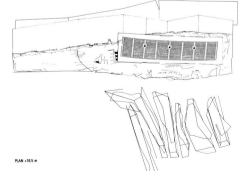

PLAN +16.5 m

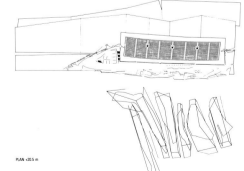

PLAN +20.5 m

18

# JANEK BIELSKI

**JANEK BIELSKI**

Education:

Bachelor of Science

University of Southern California, 1976

Diploma

Architectural Association, London, 1981

Professional Experience:

Eric Owen Moss, Architects

Ed Fine Associates

Bobrow Thomas & Associates

Louis de Soissons Partnership, London

Koulermos, Malara & Associates, Milan

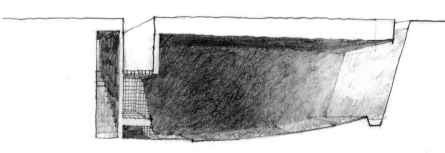

**The Desert Project** California Desert, California 1989-1990

The Desert Project is composed of three parts: the myth of dwelling in a crevice; a retreat placed on the site of a fictitious archaeological dig; and a house in the desert. The project explores the relationship between the ritualistic and formal properties of architecture in the desert.

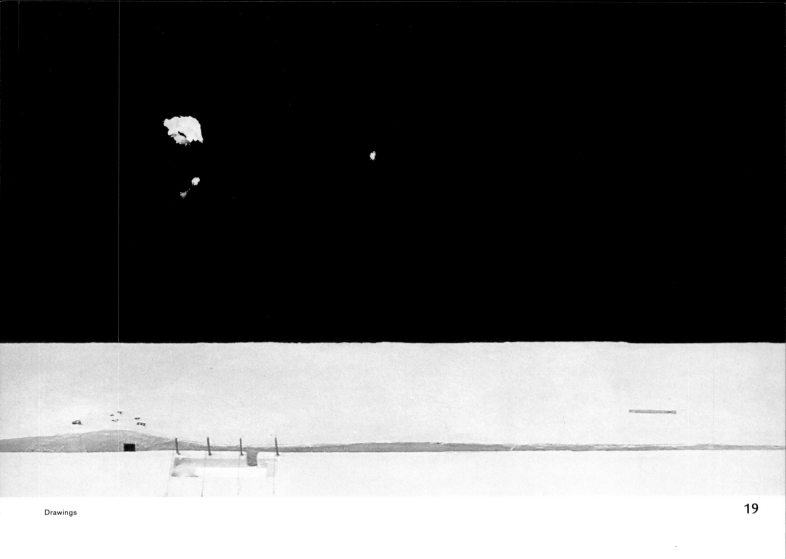

Drawings

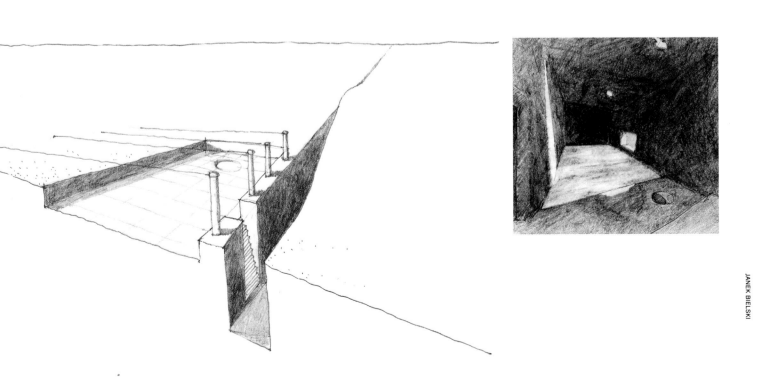

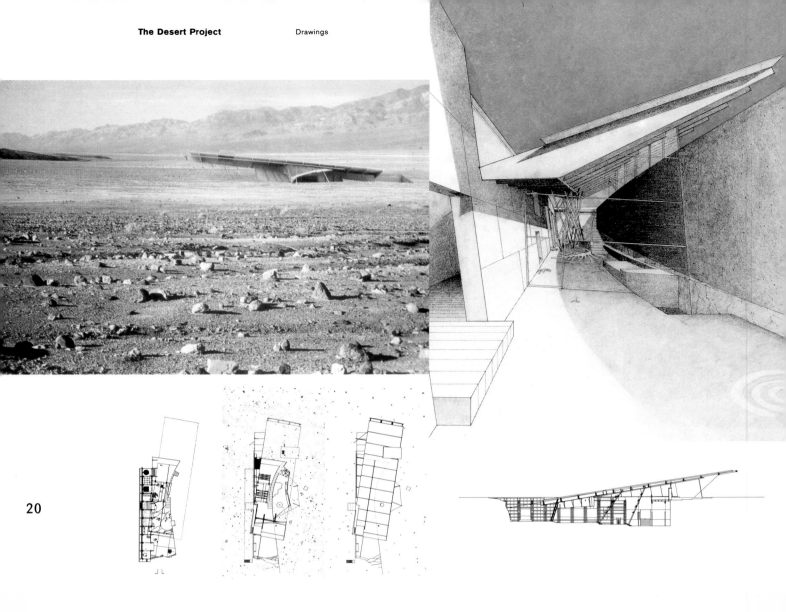

20

## Urban Mission

Los Angeles, California 1990

The project assumes that, faced with diminishing urban alternatives, various special interest groups will take control of the city in the near future and will then implement their own particular programs. Urban Mission exemplifies one such "take-over" at a Wilshire Boulevard intersection. In this case study, Franciscan monks transform the existing office buildings and convenience centers into a community inspired by Junipero Serra's California missions of the 18th century.

Models

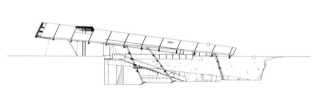

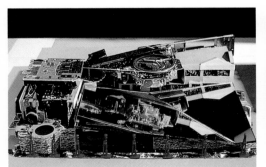

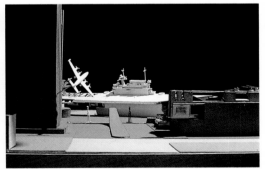

**Santa Monica House** Santa Monica, California 1986

The Santa Monica House is a box densely packed with a series of disparate events that reflect various programmatic needs. These events, including a glass-prism dining room and a meditation "nest" on the roof, physically articulate the dweller's lifestyle.

Garden elevation

Model

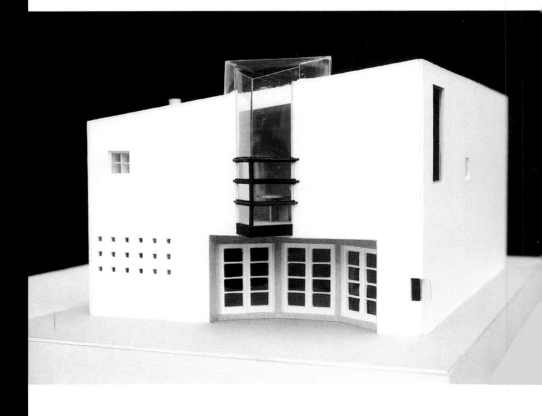

**San Fernando Valley House** San Fernando Valley, California 1987-1989

The placement of two houses on this oddly shaped lot was an attempt to increase the density of suburbs and to create a sense of community among individual houses, but without sacrificing either privacy or the idiosyncracies of a detached house.

**Red Dog Films Offices** Los Angeles, California 1989

**PERRY ANDELIN BLAKE**

Education:

Master of Architecture
Harvard University,1984
Bachelor of Architecture
Utah State, Utah, 1980

Professional Experience:

Frank O. Gehry & Associates

**ALAN KONG AU**

Education:

Master of Architecture
Cornell University
Bachelor of Industrial Design
Columbus College, Ohio, 1978

Professional Experience:

Frank O. Gehry & Associates
Glen Fleck Inc.

24

# BLAKE + AU

A series of elemental spaces highlighted with vivid color form these offices for a film production company.

Model

**Richard X Music Video Set**

Hollywood, California  1989

An expressionistic set for a rock music video employs forced perspective and powerful forms to evoke both the energy of the music and the stylistic manner in which it is presented.

Reception area

**Mambo Films Offices** Los Angeles, California 1989

Lively, but affordable, materials enliven these storefront offices for a small production company.

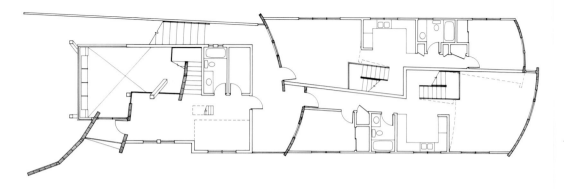

**Campbell House** Venice, California

1989-1990

A single-family home in a rough neighborhood expresses both the
freedom of beach living and concerns about security.

Plan

**Mambo Films Offices**

Interior View

29

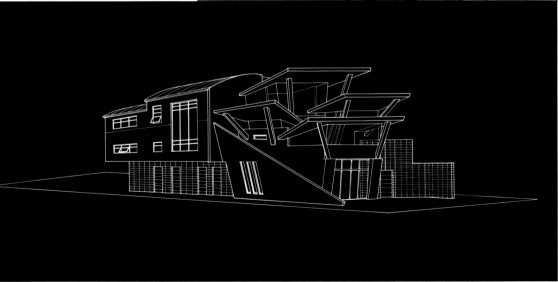

Perspective

# MICHAEL BURCH

**MICHAEL BURCH**

Education:

Bachelor of Arts in Architecture
UC Berkeley, 1975
Master of Architecture
Yale University, 1982

Professional Experience:

The Jerde Partnership
UCLA Urban Innovations Group
Skidmore, Owings & Merrill
Killingsworth, Brady & Associates

Model

**McMahon Residence Addition** Los Angeles, California 1989-1990

The expansion of this small house overlooking the Silver Lake Reservoir attempts to alter traditional divisions between public and private spaces and takes advantage of the dramatic view. The existing house is treated as a base or "ruin" out of which the purposefully modern forms of the addition emerge.

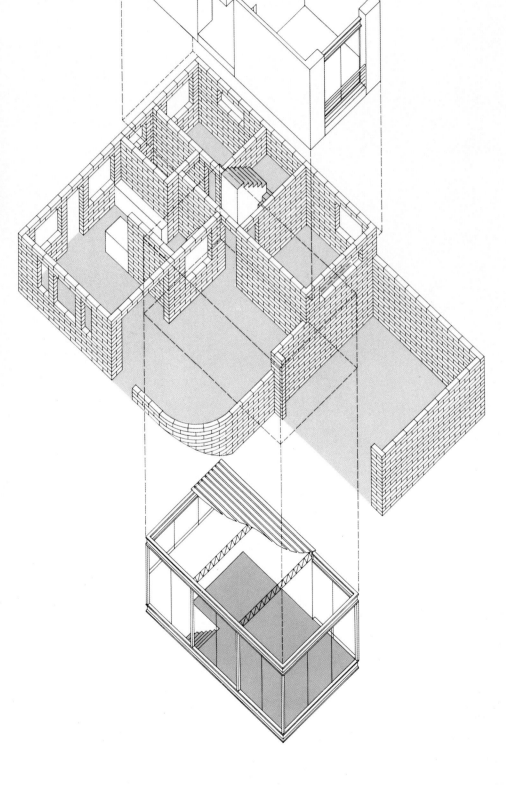

Axonometric

**Jonathan Martin, Inc.**
Los Angeles, California 1988

Jonathan Martin, a clothing manufacturer in Los Angeles, commissioned this renovation and expansion of the company's 65,000-square-foot warehouse, manufacturing facility, office building, and loading dock. The design reflects both concerns about the less-than-friendly neighborhood and the exuberance of the fashion industry.

32

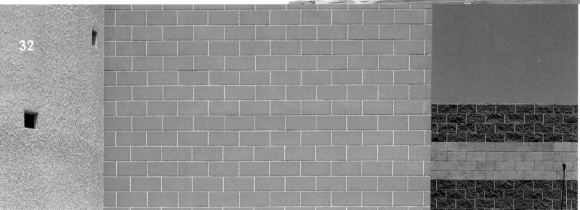

Detail of cladding material

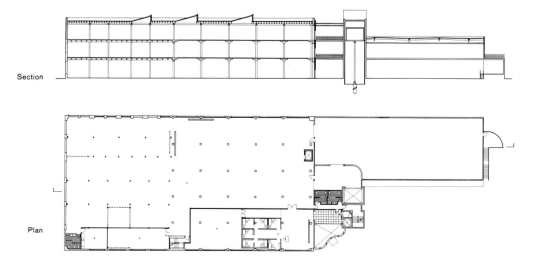

Section

Plan

View from loading dock

Office area

Fire stairs

33

MICHAEL BURCH

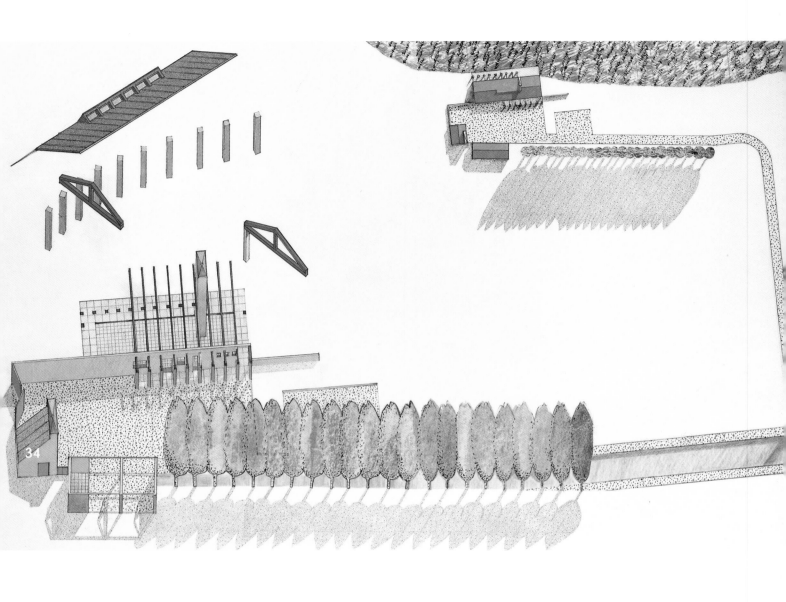

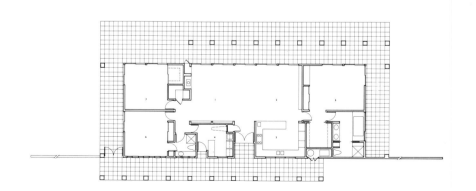

**Hampton Ranch House** Hickman, California 1990

Plan

Set among the orchards and fields of the Central Valley, this residence for a rancher and his wife also
includes a bunkhouse for guests, a carport and a tack room.  The hard plaster walls, punched openings, metal
roof and pergolas make reference to the local vernacular.

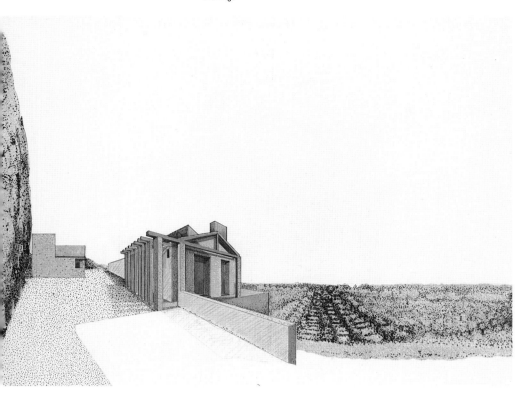

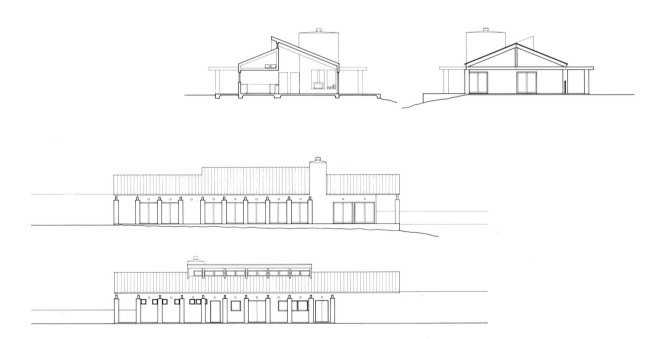

Section/Elevation

# VICTORIA CASASCO

**VICTORIA CASASCO**

Education:

Bachelor of Fine Arts
Rhode Island School
of Design, 1978
Master of Architecture
Columbia University, 1983

Professional Experience:

Arquitectonica
Duany & Plater-Zyberk
Robert A. M. Stern

Entrance detail

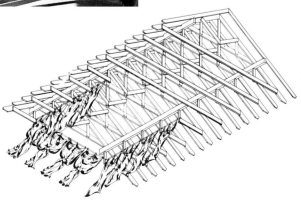

Truss detail

**Appell Residence** Seaside, Florida  1988-1989

The Appell Residence explores the possibilities of living spaces that blur the boundaries between indoors and outdoors. Exterior wood siding and interior plywood wall surfaces are treated as skins which are superimposed over a skeletal frame.

Elevations

37

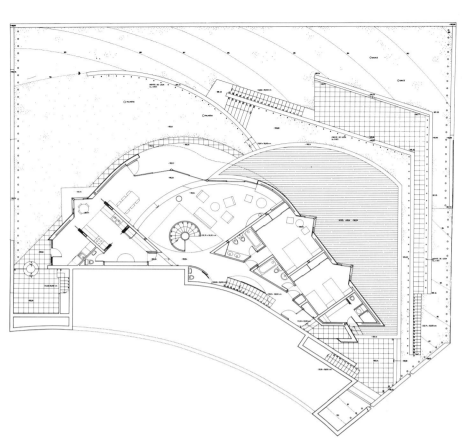

**Aznar Residence**

(with Carlos Garcia-Delgado)

Barcelona, Spain 1987-90

38

The Aznar house is a study in organic form using curved walls of poured concrete set against large bands of glass. This house is sited on a hillside above Barcelona, and it is intended to merge into the larger surrounding landscape.

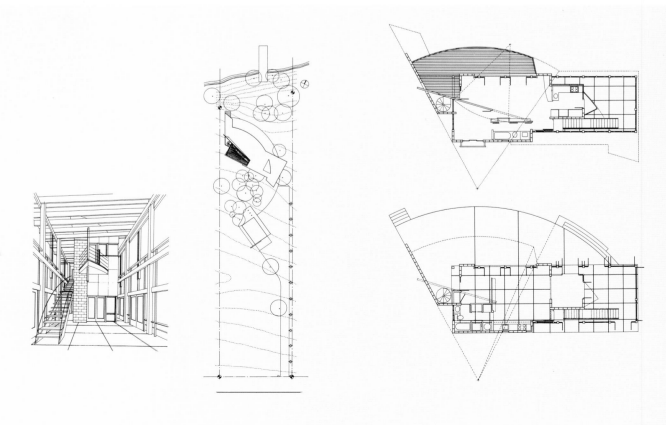

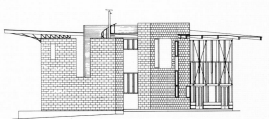

**Kaye Residence** Gulf Coast, Florida  1987-1991

The Kaye Residence is divided into two equal parts: an exterior screened enclosure and an interior volume of equal dimensions. The first- and second-level interior spaces are treated as separate entities connected at either end by exterior stairs.

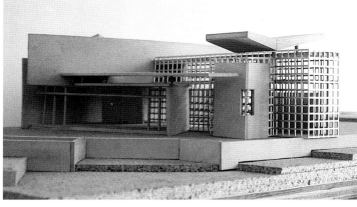

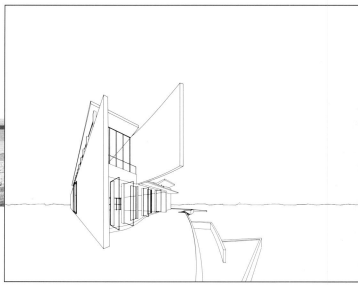

Details

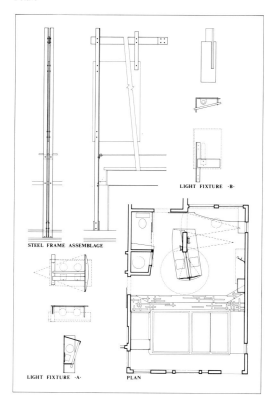

**Booth Bathing Chamber** Santa Monica, California  1989

The Booth Bathing Chamber began as a simple intervention into an existing 17 x 23-foot bathroom, but was developed both conceptually and symbolically as an art installation. All of the bathroom's elements were designed to be dismounted, moved, and re-erected if the existing house were to be demolished.

40

**Booth Residence** Santa Monica, California 1991

The Booth Residence contrasts an exposed steel structure with the organic shapes of enclosing stone walls.
The grid opens up the house to create extensions of interior spaces into verandas, while the building's massive
forms gesture toward views of the Pacific Ocean and the adjacent canyon site.

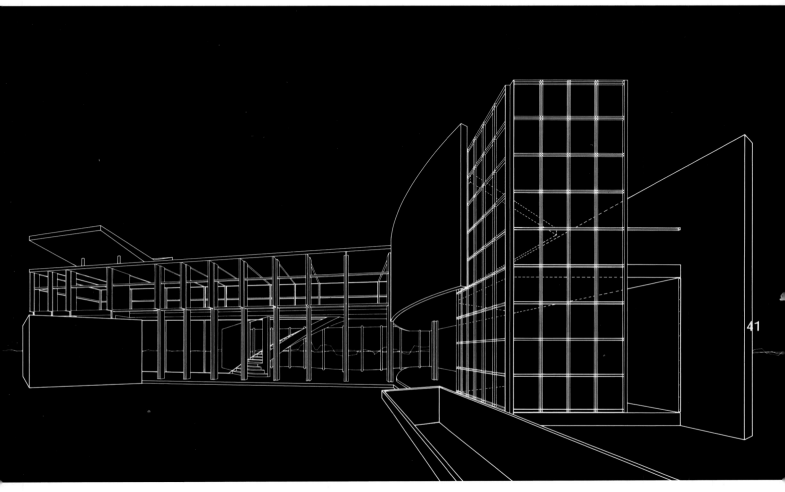

41

Perspective

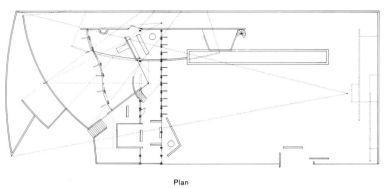

Plan

VICTORIA CASASCO

# BUILDING

## ( in ) THE

By Aaron Betsky

## BRAVE NEW WORLD

The landscape of Southern California is all but devoid of monuments in a traditional sense. In the same sense, it is also without a clearly defined vernacular. Man has not elaborated the natural conditions of this semi-arid terrain into decorative orders, nor has he built memorials to his achievements in subjugating it. The architecture of Southern California exists largely outside of the realm of the age-old contest with nature that turns building into an act either of the imposition of alien human form or of the mediation of natural forces. Instead, architecture here has been conceived of as an artifact at the end of the line, a technological invention.

Such statements, however, can only be made while whizzing by the multitudinous complexities of this city. In reality, Southern California is no Eden for architectural rebirth, where one can pluck the oranges of a post-Descartian architecture from holographic trees nurtured by pumped-in intellects. It is a city like any other, where a vast majority of practitioners affirm the existing social and economic status quo through the design of pointless buildings, while a small group of mainly young designers tries to figure out how to create an alternative to such a practice. At the same time, the absence of controlling devices, such as development patterns connected to history, an untainted natural landscape, or objects that have become cultural and social focal points, is indeed liberating.

Los Angeles lacks a clear civic architecture. Its government is housed in buildings undistinguishable from the surrounding office buildings, its cultural institutions are broken apart into fragmented, almost invisible, pavilions. The so-called civic center of downtown Los Angeles has only one true focal point — city hall. This modest skyscraper, however, is not at the end of any clear axis, but sits outside of the major thrust of development and is dwarfed by surrounding boxes created in the 1950s to house bureaucracies. The latest government building, the Ronald Reagan State Building, continues this tradition through dissolution into multiple towers enmeshed in a globular base eaten out by the requisite atrium space. Even the much-vaunted Pasadena Civic Center has lost its major axis, while the city hall there is a stage set of civic rhetoric that is essentially hollow: the tower is empty, and the solid front of the building is in fact a thin shell wrapped around a courtyard. The Los Angeles County Museum of Art is a series of pavilions hiding behind a large billboard, while the Museum of Contemporary Art is buried in a parking structure so as not to obscure the view from the surrounding office buildings that paid for its construction.

There are, however, alternative focal points in the Los Angeles landscape: oil derricks, freeway overpasses, pleasure piers, and the Hollywood sign. Yet all of these monumental markers are essentially meaningless. They are enigmatic results of systems of communication, of marketing needs, or of the extraction of something invisible. Large community *foci* such as shopping centers turn inward, leaving only mute scaffolding for the clothing racks inside to face the adoring sea of parked cars. Skyscrapers, which in cities like New York perform a monumental function, are here cut off from the life of the street, entered through labyrinthine parking garages, and decapitated by a law that mandates helicopter landing pads on top of all tall buildings. The result is a city organized around roads and signs, not solid objects that indicate the aspirations, memories, or self-image of a community.

But what about the field around these objects? Wouldn't the vernacular richness of daily experience more than make up for the lack of a grand architecture? Yet it is hard to find a Los Angeles vernacular. In response to the climate, buildings here have a tendency to turn inward, leaving lush vegetation in place of facades. That gesture is about as close as the city comes to an architectonic response to its geography. The remaining elements of its vernacular are a grab bag of wholly imported styles, including the fragments of an international style slapped together in ephemeral constructions that are either torn down or remodeled before they can accrue memories. There is a vernacular in terms of frequently repeated compositional patterns that are generated wholly by the economic pressures on them: the dingbat apartment block, the fast-food stand, the strip shopping mall. Yet these building blocks of a Los Angeles vernacular, however glorified by the lovers of the architecture during the 1950s, do not reflect the need of their inhabitants and are generally not specific to their site. They are created because of economic necessity and are essentially mass-produced. If they are expressions of the nature of Los Angeles, they are so only negatively, as the lowest common denominator of design, affordable given the tremendous development pressures on almost every site in the city. The resulting evanescence of the man-made landscape is furthered by the continually changing population of the Basin, which is quickly becoming the most ethnically diverse in the world. There are few communities that do not dissolve before one generation has a chance to grow up, whether under the pressures of development or because of the mobility of its own population.

The only constant in man-made Los Angeles is technology. Like all cities, Los Angeles is built on vast and usually invisible systems of infrastructure of irrigation, electricity, sewage, communication, and transportation. But where in other cities a bend in the road might recall the memory of an old stream bed, in Los Angeles it is the result of the meeting of two different subdevelopments, and a major intersection is the result of a long forgotten juncture between two streetcar lines. The availability of water is not commemorated in bridges or fountains, but only in the greenness of lawns. The places where infrastructure erupts form the only causes for architectonic focal points in Los Angeles. Freeway exit ramps are increasingly ringed with castellated commercial developments; the arrival of water from the Owens Valley occasions a grand set of concrete forms cascading down the Grapevine Pass; and electrical substations send out their ganglia of wires from a spider's web of sparkling power. Freeways form street walls at a larger scale, while the military installations that ring the Southland create its true gateways and mark the limits of its growth. Technology is the preeminent definer of the forms of Los Angeles.

The result of such conditions is that here, more than in most cities, the notion of an independent architectural object seems slightly absurd, as does the notion of either monumental form or a well-worn vernacular. Attempts to glorify the signs and symbols of technology to turn them into a system of monuments and monumental open spaces deny the essential character of these enablers of artifice, namely their nature as scaffolding, not form. This does not mean that there is no possibility for architecture in Los Angeles. It just indicates the need for letting go of the idea that architecture is a solid mediator between individuals, or between individuals and nature. The climate has already invalidated the latter, while the historical place of Los Angeles as the end of the road, the haven of exiles, and the dreamland where manifest destiny can be constructed, has made short shrift of the former.

What we are left with is a bricolage whose true symbol is Watts Towers, a meaningless monument pieced together from cast-off elements. We are left with communities parachuted into the desert, isolated from each other, constructed from the most shoddy materials, and open to continual change. What we are left with is a city that will soon be the largest industrial base in the country, sprawling into an endless sea of tilt-up sweatshops, whose accumulated wealth has not and will not coalesce into any permanent form that will give it identity, but will instead disappear into the ever-spiraling worth of the landscape itself. What we are left with is a new kind of semidesert, a man-made landscape so extensive that it deserves that name.

In Southern California, technology has created a completely artificial alternative to the natural world. Here, streams are buried in concrete culverts, or exchanged for the sluggish rivers of the freeways, which gather into pools and waterfalls at crucial intersections. The surrounding mountains, so tall and absolute as to defy human comprehension, become a datum line visible only on a few clear days, and soon they too will only be interruptions in the sprawl, containing no remnants of castles or pleasure gardens. Our new mountains are magic ones in Disneyland, or they are formed by the accumulation of activity that pushes buildings up in concentric, if somewhat erratic, rings around freeway intersections. This new landscape is harsh and inimical, a hostile environment where you have to learn how to burrow down or under to discover the sustenance buried in the rich interiors of homes, stores, or restaurants. The features of this landscape are hard to distinguish from the surroundings, and appear monotonous to the untrained eye, but, as in the desert, they reveal themselves to the trained eye as the crucial markers in dangerous terrain. Even the hues of our pollution mimic the rich ochers, purples, and browns that build up the subtle palette of the desert.

The progeny of this desert appear slightly surreal to one accustomed to more temperate climates. They are prickly, hard, and without the kind of gradual ascension from base to top that marks a well-rounded tree or plant. They are often deformed by their specific function or type, and they are extremely inward-oriented, protecting themselves from all enemies and storing up their precious resources. They are either minute and brightly colored, or vast and muted. Their spiky forms often take on the appearance of armor plating, or of an armory of defensive weapons.

Of course, they are just the buildings or the plants. The true inhabitants are the nomads, those who cannot rest in the desert, but must search continually for water or, in the case of Los Angeles, for something more ephemeral to keep them going: the future, always out of reach. That future is the very engine of modernization, that which fuels the rise in prices, the influx of immigrants, and the physical sprawl of the city itself. It is symbolized by the Pacific Ocean, the unconquered West towards which the multimillion dollar homes that line the coast turn their plate-glass eyes adoringly: it's out there, somewhere past the sunset, under the water, beyond the water, beyond the edge. The modern nomads, meanwhile, are not quite human anymore. They have been married to their technological devices. In Los Angeles, you really need your sunglasses. You really shouldn't breathe unfiltered air. You need your air conditioning. You need your car. The inhabitants of the Los Angeles deserts are a kind of satyr—half-human, half-machine.

First, the densification of Los Angeles is changing the more amorphous, spread-out character of the city. Over 50,000 people in Los Angeles live in garages. Two-story apartment buildings are making way for four-story condominiums. Downtown is developing into a dense core. Taken together, these developments should make the city look more urbane. Yet this replication of the larger grids at a smaller scale and the filling-out of fragmentary forms into larger non-wholes in fact intensifies the confusion. It is now almost impossible to create isolated objects. Architecture in Los Angeles, as in most other cities, has become a question of transforming the laws, regulations, and structures of the city. Here the game seems only more abstract and absurd, given the current and deracinated nature of the so-called context to be addressed by the architect. The chaotic nature of the city becomes more evident, and thus one could say its destiny as the first city beyond the bounds of reason, and thus of humanistic urban planning, seems ever more imminent.

Second, this tendency towards post-humanism is not to be understood as necessarily bad. In fact, making value judgments about such developments is dangerous since it leads to the proposal of the kind of "solutions" that have pockmarked our cities with well-intentioned disasters. An attempt to understand the nature of the evolution of humanity beyond the definitions established by seventeenth-century rationalism might be of greater interest, and in fact Los Angeles could act as a laboratory for the development of methods of critical evaluation as much as it can create new and interesting mutations of form. Such an approach does not absolve architecture, whether as a drawn or built construction, from its responsibility to take a political stance, that is, to participate actively in the development of the city in such a way as to prevent the complete abrogation of rights by those in control of its physical resources. Rather, it is the role of the architects to create compelling visions of transformation that can be erected against the purely destructive forces inherent in the economic and social structure of the city.

Finally, nature always threatens to reassert itself as a defining factor. The earthquake faults are near, and periodically send out their warning tremors. Much of the architecture of Los Angeles is, in fact, deformed by anticipation of "the big one," so that the old role of architecture as a bastion against a post-Edenic world sneaks in through the earthquake codes. Less dramatically, water remains scarce, and the fear of its disappearance gives an edge to those who wish to place artificial limits on the development of the metropolis. Yet, to those willing to keep dreaming, the Pacific once again is the future — an endless horizon of water waiting to be transformed into sustenance for the man-made desert.

Given such a daunting landscape, how are young architects performing? First of all, they are building on an indigenous tradition. Architects have been making sense out of the seeming chaos of Los Angeles. In fact, one might argue that they have found themselves confronted with processes of modernization before many other cities and, as a result, have developed a more pronounced modernism. Irving Gill's reductivist aesthetic — based on the sparse anonymity of whatever local vernacular was still present at the turn of the century, and married to the inexorable logic of tilt-up construction — predated the more affected form of the Viennese heroes of classical modernism. Schindler, building on the work of the Greene brothers, created an architecture expressive

of the lack of a center, static dividers, or the object quality of local form. The Case Study program of the 1950s produced kits of parts that were meant to integrate architecture into the technological marvel that had created this modern metropolis out of defense industries, romantic illusions, and available land. Frank Gehry later synthesized much of this city into enigmatic objects that refuse to complete themselves or to make sense. Most recently, the former employers of many of those whose work is collected here, such as Thom Mayne and Michael Rotondi, Craig Hodgetts and Robert Mangurian, Eric Moss, or Frank Israel, have been struggling to create an architecture that either draws on research by artists into the relationship between artifice and experience, or which transforms itself into set design at an urban scale. The vitality of their work is a testimony to the fact that Los Angeles does produce architecture which at its best does not look like building, but is an abstract interruption in the city, a piece of technology honed for living, or a self-consciously vivid set for modern living.

The work of the younger generation builds on these traditions, but is also informed by more classical notions of architecture that these designers, all but a few of whom grew up and were educated elsewhere, brought with them to California. Their visions can be said to oscillate between two ideal images of man, not including that of the da Vincian Renaissance hero squaring the circle and thus resolving the conflict between man in nature in favor of man's projective, abstracting capabilities. Rather, one finds the image of the naked man first postulated by Schindler, released from nature, standing naked on the shore of the Pacific. The inhabitant of the ramshackle beach shack, the surfer, is the prototype of this new man, and his undressing is mirrored in the unclothing of structure started by Schindler and brought to full flower by Frank Gehry. This new Adam is the conceptual client of what might be called the *Gehry-schule*, an ever-growing group of young designers who either worked for, or moved to the city because of the reputation of, "the godfather of the Los Angeles avant-garde." The other model is the man/machine satyr, depicted at the end of the first *Star Trek* motion picture and consummated in what Elizabeth Diller has called "an architecture of prosthetics." This satyr is served by another school, this one focused around the Southern California Institute of Architecture and the work of Morphosis. Between these two poles stretch the tentative assemblages of built and drawn form that are the oeuvre of a new generation of Los Angeles architects.

On one side of the spectrum are the new primitives—the Los Angeles branch of a national movement back to the ranch, back to basics, and back to materials. Produced by those who assimilated the teaching of the Italian and South American rationalists such as Mario Gandelsonas and Jorge Silvetti during the 1970s and 1980s, and who then applied the new reductive, memory-driven forms to a perceived American vernacular, their work relies heavily on simple, geometric shapes, cubical volumes, uncluttered planes, and a fondness for concrete, concrete-colored stucco, and concrete block, held together by a muscular armature of metal trusses, window surrounds, and roofs. This is architecture pushed back to a defensive position, a desperate attempt to make monuments in a world that does not need them. Where such work succeeds is in its very anguish. In Los Angeles, however, such monumental commentary often becomes as ironic and wistful as its neo-Spanish, stage-set civic centers, except that the methods of destabilization are here distinctly modern. The stark planes are undercut, float in space, or are skewed to activate the grand volumes. Architecture is reduced to almost nothing, but that small something threatens to destabilize the whole, and thus creates an appropriate strategy of subversion.

The plot thickens with the emergence of forms that are joyfully thin and highly colored. Several of the young architects working in Los Angeles delight in the cheapness, mass production, and blandness of the basic building blocks of architecture here, but only because the material is so pliable. In the end, they produce sophisticated gestures without any content. Their colorful cutoffs are just active participants in the city, except that these actors are stripped down, muscular, and thus more powerful than the dainty forms all around them. This is architecture for the brightly colored, well-toned denizens of Gold's Gym and Muscle Beach, except that the client turns out to be an "industry" executive writing the script of his own life.

This mixture of stripping and acting, the reliance on the expressiveness of malleable materials, and the creation of a more muscular, honest dance of basic forms in a city of affectations are the hallmarks of the work of many from the *Gehry-schule*. Working with the tortured forms and telescoping volumes of the master, they push his undressing of the basic forms of the city one step further, creating haunting fragments of drywall, stud walls, roof planes, and skylights that dance away from convention. Unadorned and clad in only the most minimal materials, this work starts to take on some of the quick-cut, pan-shot, fast-edit character of a music video. Beyond Gehry's sculptural honesty, born in the Venice Beach culture of the 1960s, lies the polymorphous perversity so apparent on today's beaches.

Some of the most creative work in Los Angeles, in fact, mixes its metaphors, combining the dance of perverted forms with an interest in the grids of technology that can hold it all together. This is indeed a kind of prosthetic architecture. For many young designers, Los Angeles is the site of an archaeology where they find both the kind of abstract, molded forms of the desert and the mountains, and the mass-produced frames and connections that turn the endless suburbs into a formless web of technologically defined habitation. This is work that is ambivalent about whether it prefers the man-made or the natural desert, but this indecision seems to vitiate, rather than incapacitate, the work. Narrative replaces program for young architects of a more theoretical bent, and in these stories architecture becomes the transformation of what is already there—a landscaping job rather than the erection of hopeful new edifices of human reason. Beyond stripping down and getting back to Adam, architects here see the possibility for rewriting the history of The Fall as a new Genesis.

Beyond such multiple strategies, many of which

have been adapted at various times by several of the architects shown here, there are those who have a more focused notion of the role of architecture in the city. Those that I would call technomorphists accept the man-made landscape as a given and merely want to create the appropriate form for a world of post-humanistic artifice. To them, the world is an uncertain and vaguely threatening place where the solace of good forms has no place. By emphasizing the working of machined surfaces and by mimicking the human body in their buildings, they make the machinery of the city into the image of man, while creating a mechanized man at the scale of the city. When they create objects, they are not so much buildings as giant machines. Ominous and overwhelming, these mechanical beasts have come to replace the human body with something larger and more sophisticated, but still imbued with a dream of conscious control over reality. This is work that delights in the dawn of a fully technological landscape, that glorifies the many machines that are necessary to survive on that seemingly arid plain, and that actively seeks the disappearance of the solid forms with which we are so familiar. Gleaming and dangerous, their forms promise something beyond comfort, as uncertain as their theories of chaos.

The work of the design firms shown here, as well as that of countless other young practitioners, stretches between the naked forms of the new primitives and the humanoid machines of the technomorphists. Nothing ties their work together except that they live in the peculiar design laboratory of Los Angeles. Their designs are, therefore, conscious of the technological deformations of the human landscape. Their forms are almost all tortured, deformed, and skewed by this consciousness. They are resolutely modernist in their faith in the ability to construct an alternative physical framework that both refuses to accept the constraints of the memory of tradition and projects us into an unknown future that validates our current activities. It is an architecture produced in a city that has invented itself. The work is local in that it delights in raw building materials that have never coalesced into either monuments or a vernacular. Instead, it closes itself into enigmatic,

surreal, or purely defensive gestures against the man-made desert. What is preserved inside these forms is, as often as not, light. The very abundance of sun that has created the desert is turned into an excuse for a concentration on the kind of perceptual self-consciousness pioneered by the "light and space" artists of the 1960s, so that the human ability to experience is cultivated even within technology. Even when such optimism is replaced by the dark forms of technology, a faith remains that, beyond the creation of isolated objects, but within Los Angeles, and through the transformation of the physical conditions in which we live, an architecture can be found, projected, and constructed.

**RON GOLAN**

Education:

Bachelor of Architecture
California Polytechnic State University
San Luis Obispo, 1981
Master of Architecture
Southern California Institute of
Architecture, 1986

Professional Experience:

Pike/Gentry Associates
Design Engineering Systems
Martin Schmidt, Architect,
Carona, Switzerland

**ERIC A. KAHN**

Education:

Bachelor of Architecture
California Polytechnic State University
San Luis Obispo, 1981

Professional Experience:

SuperStudio, Florence
Morphosis
Skidmore, Owings & Merrill

**RUSSELL N. THOMSEN**

Education:

Bachelor of Architecture
California Polytechnic State University
San Luis Obispo, 1981

Professional Experience:

SuperStudio, Florence
Mark Mack, Architect
Richard Meier, Architect

50

# CENTRAL OFFICE OF ARCHITECTURE

**Brix Restaurant**

Venice, California 1990

The Brix Restaurant project involved the remodeling of a 1,300-square-foot facility located in a highly chaotic commercial fabric. A large, perforated metal screen hovers between the street and the building, heightening the presence of the small restaurant and filtering much of the street's visual chaos from the interior.

51

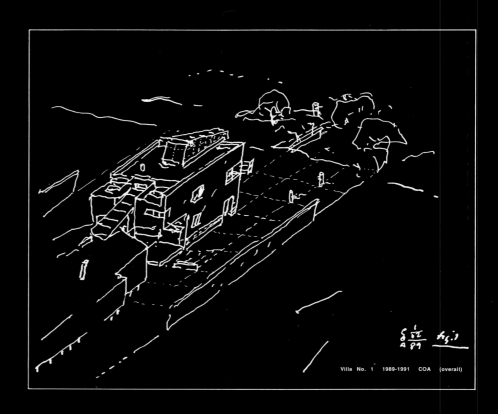

Villa No. 1    1989-1991    COA    (overall)

**Kahn Residence** Los Angeles, California    1989-1991

The Kahn Residence consists of a 2,000-square-foot addition to a
house in Pacific Palisades. The existing house was treated as a found
object. The new addition then becomes a series of distinct elements

which address different aspects of the site. A sheet-metal garage
contrasts with a concrete-block box containing the major living
elements of the house. The new second floor of this block affords
views of the canyon and the ocean.

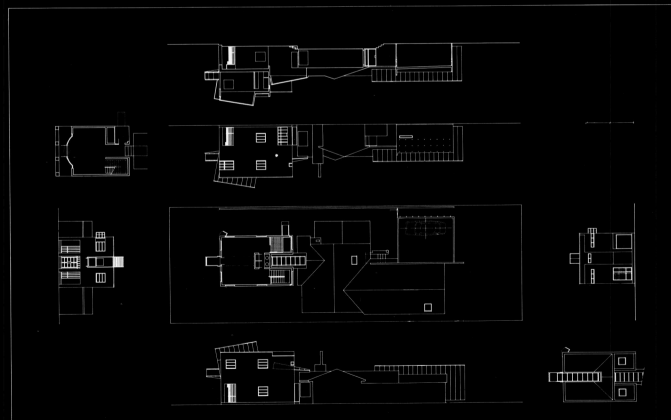

Villa No. 1  1989-1991  COA  (detail)

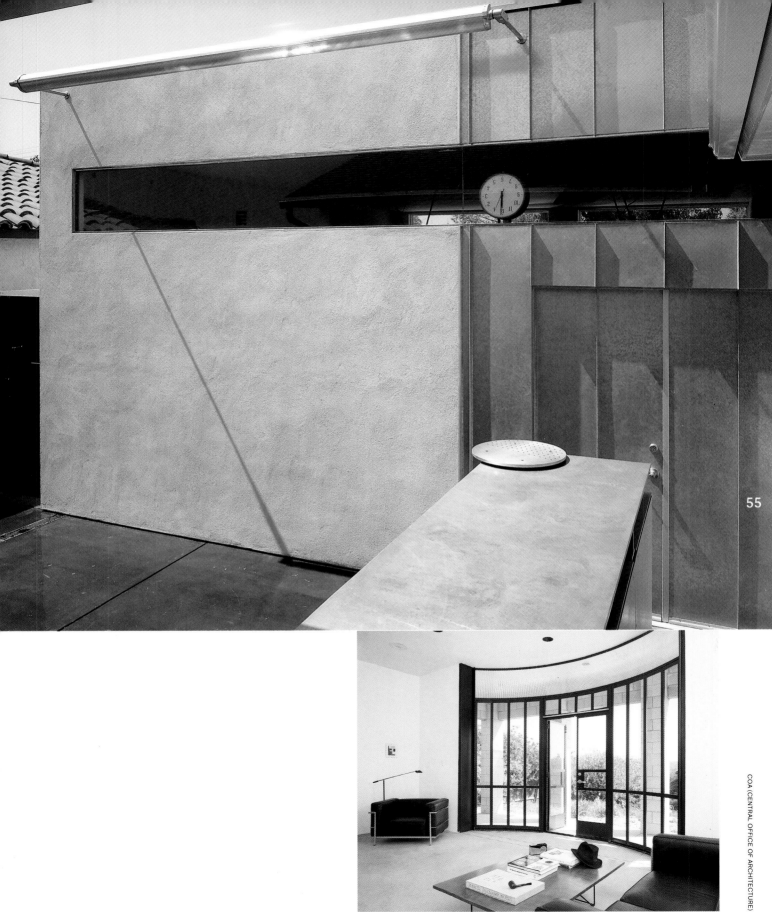

55

**"SiteWorks: Investigations of the Inbetween"**
Los Angeles, California
1990

This project was a commissioned proposal by the UCLA Architecture Journal for an exhibition held at the School of Architecture and Urban Planning at the University of California, Los Angeles, in June 1990. The exhibit presented various explorations into the potential of residual spaces within the city of Los Angeles.

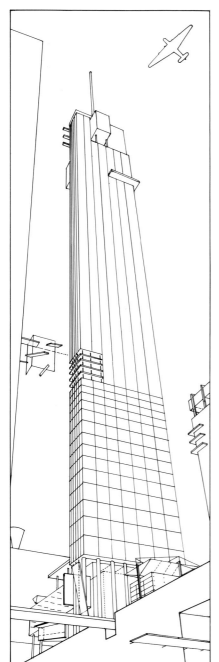

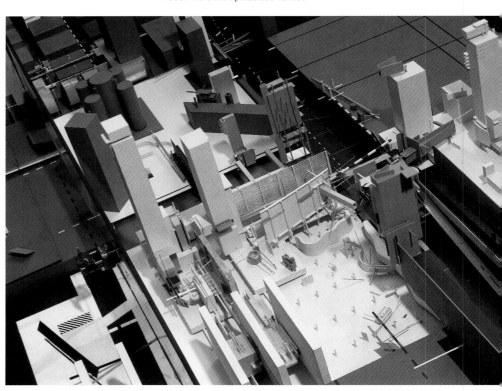

Model

Site plan

Sections

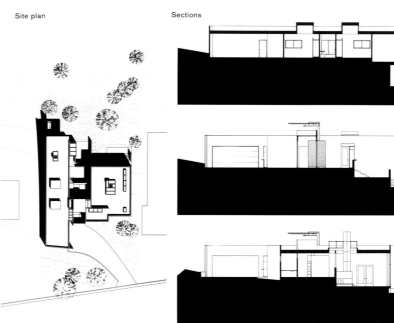

**Poteet Residence**
Glendale, California  1989-1992

This project consists of a 3,500-square-foot residence for an art collector and his family located on a sloping wooded suburban site. The public spaces exist within a single open volume as a free-plan arrangement, defined by level changes and walls of varying heights.

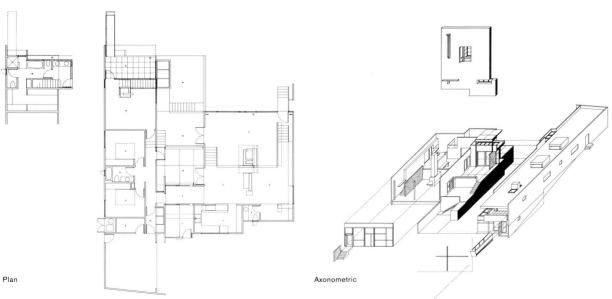

Plan

Axonometric

COA (CENTRAL OFFICE OF ARCHITECTURE)

# NEIL M. DENARI

**Prototype landscapes** 1990

These three drawings represent projects that are part of an ongoing investigation of the urban landscape of America. A technology that brings out the intrinsic, but usually hidden, nature of certain sites and modes of transportation acts as the theme to these projects.

**NEIL M. DENARI**

Education:

Bachelor of Architecture
University of Houston, 1980
Master of Architecture
Harvard University, 1982

Professional Experience:

James Stewart Polshek & Partners

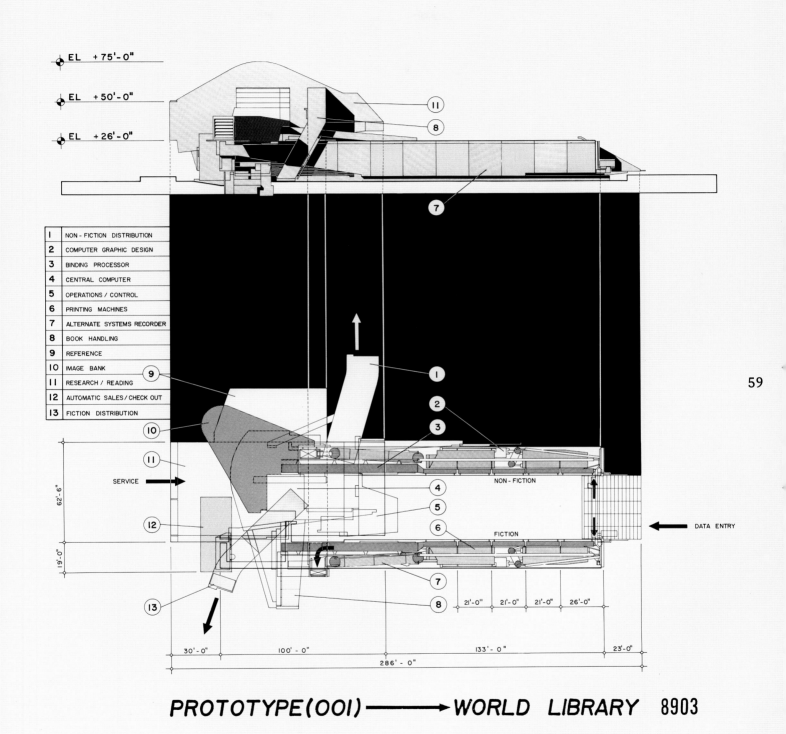

EL +75'-0"

EL +50'-0"

EL +26'-0"

| | |
|---|---|
| 1 | NON - FICTION DISTRIBUTION |
| 2 | COMPUTER GRAPHIC DESIGN |
| 3 | BINDING PROCESSOR |
| 4 | CENTRAL COMPUTER |
| 5 | OPERATIONS / CONTROL |
| 6 | PRINTING MACHINES |
| 7 | ALTERNATE SYSTEMS RECORDER |
| 8 | BOOK HANDLING |
| 9 | REFERENCE |
| 10 | IMAGE BANK |
| 11 | RESEARCH / READING |
| 12 | AUTOMATIC SALES / CHECK OUT |
| 13 | FICTION DISTRIBUTION |

59

SERVICE

62'-6"

19'-0"

NON - FICTION

FICTION

DATA ENTRY

21'-0"  21'-0"  21'-0"  26'-0"

30'-0"    100'-0"    133'-0"    23'-0"

286'-0"

PROTOTYPE(OOI) ⟶ WORLD LIBRARY 8903

NEIL DENARI

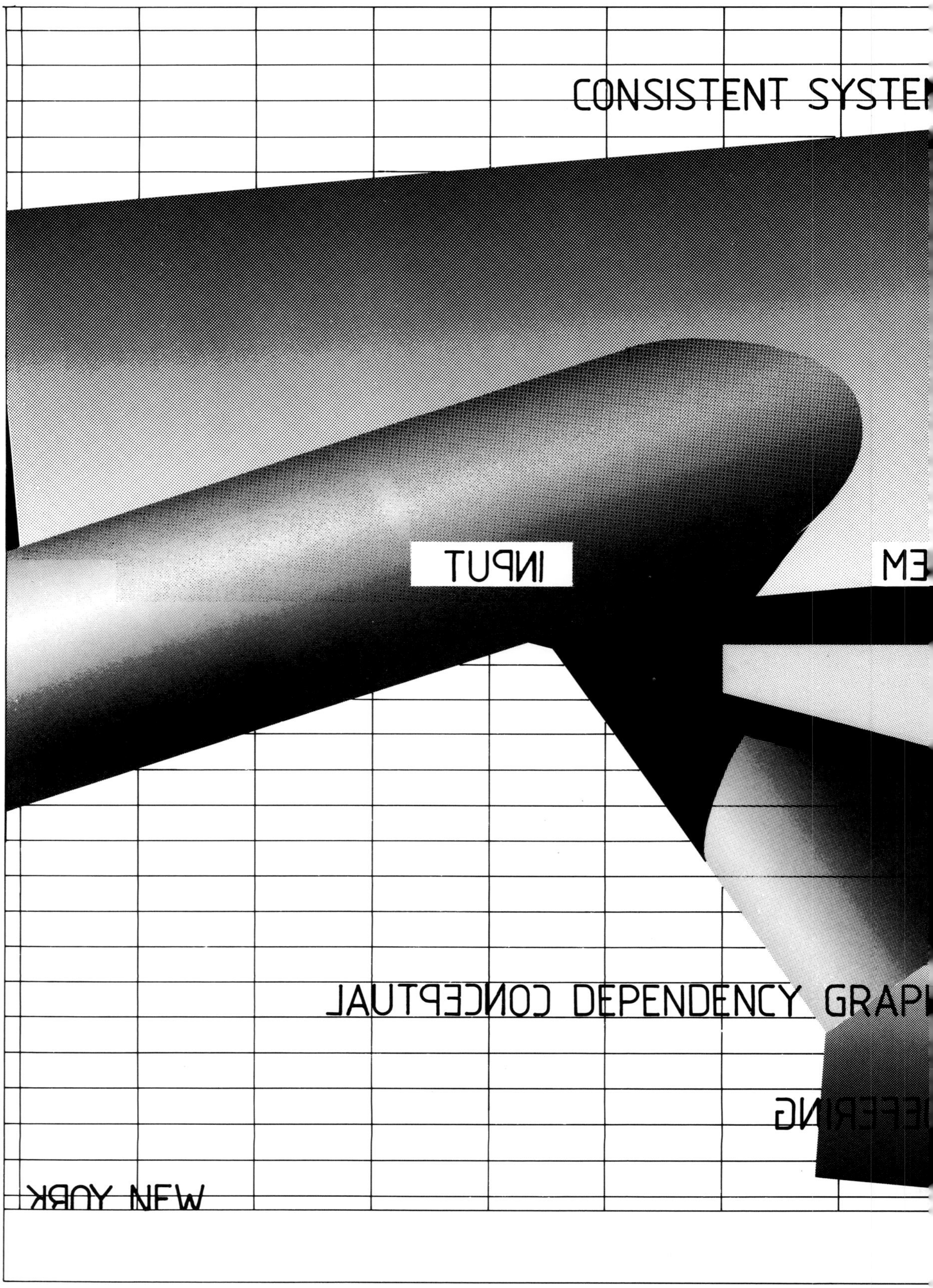

CONSISTENT SYSTEM

INPUT

EM

CONCEPTUAL DEPENDENCY GRAPH

EERING

NEW YORK

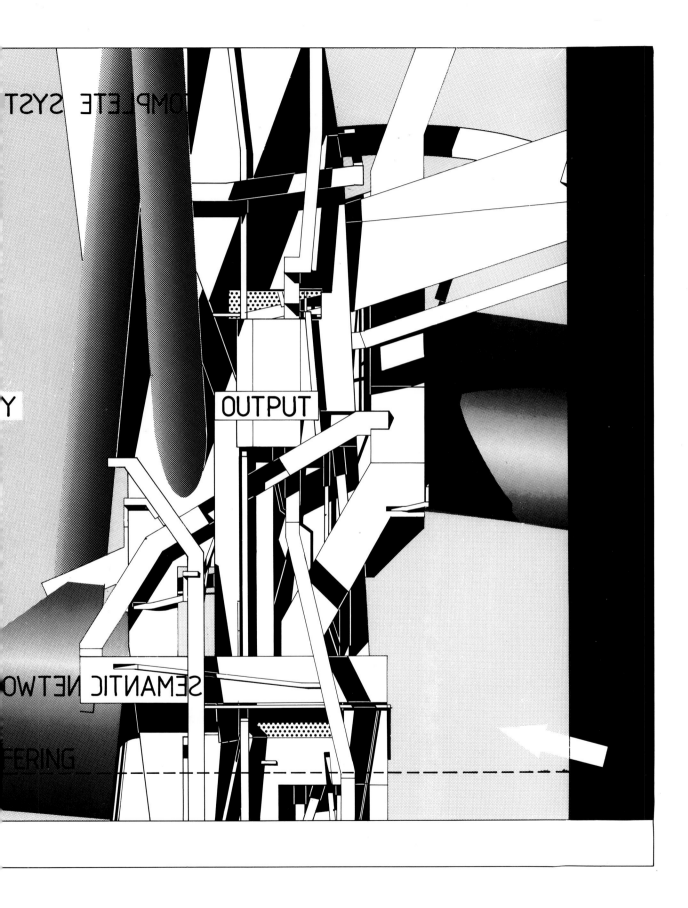

OUTPUT

OMPLETE SYST

SYST

Y

SEMANTIC NETWO

OWTEN

FERING

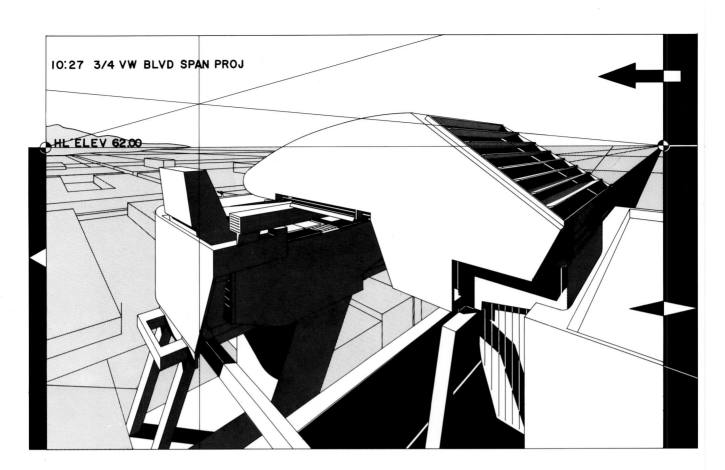

10:27 3/4 VW BLVD SPAN PROJ

HL ELEV 62.00

Perspectives

62

**Theoretical Project #9005**
Southern California   1990

This project addresses the linear
conditions and almost edgeless
boundaries of the Southern
California topography.  Mountain
ranges, valley floors, and the
coastline arbitrate the continuity
of the infinite, horizontal city.
Isolated building-objects amplify
these disturbances and are used
as "views" into a schematic, yet
atmospheric, description of
Los Angeles, hypothesizing a
scenographic mapping of
the environment.

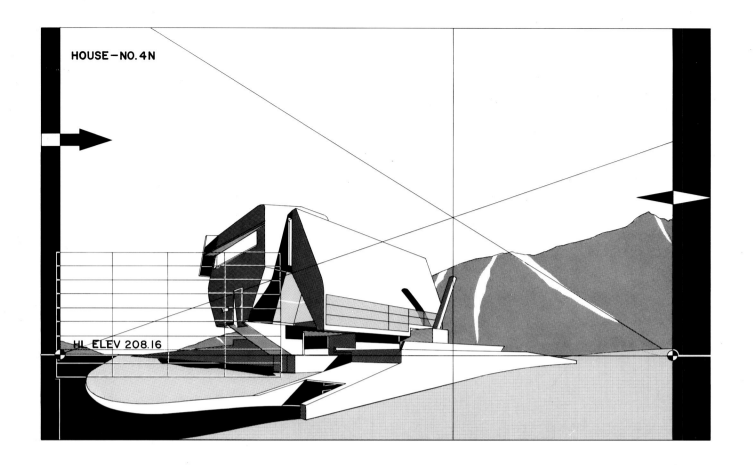

HL ELEV 208.16

63

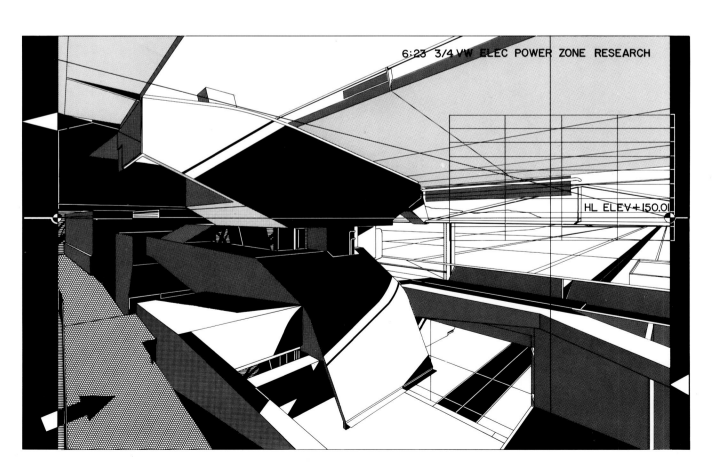

6:23 3/4 VW ELEC POWER ZONE RESEARCH

HL ELEV +150.01

NEIL DENARI

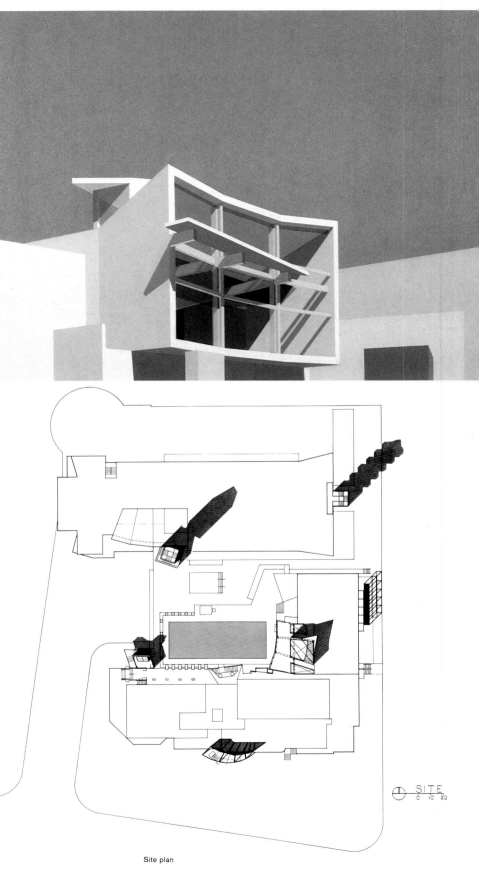

Perspective

# GUTHRIE + BURESH

**TOM J. BURESH**

Education:

Bachelor of Arts in Architecture
Iowa State University,
College of Design, 1978
Master of Architecture
UCLA Graduate School of Architecture
and Urban Planning, 1985

Professional Experience:

Frank O. Gehry & Associates
Skidmore, Owings & Merrill
Franklin D. Israel Design Associates
Studio Works, Robert Mangurian, Architect
George Miers & Associates
Flood, Meyer, Sutton & Associates
Edward Carson Beall & Associates

**DANELLE GUTHRIE BURESH**

Education:

Bachelor of Arts in Architecture
UC Berkeley, 1981
Master of Architecture
UCLA Graduate School of Architecture
and Urban Planning, 1985

Professional Experience:

Frank O. Gehry & Associates
Eugene Kupper, Architect
Studio Works, Robert Mangurian, Architect
Franklin D. Israel Design Associates
Hawley & Peterson, Architects

Site plan

Interior perspective

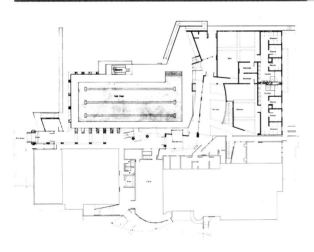

First floor plan

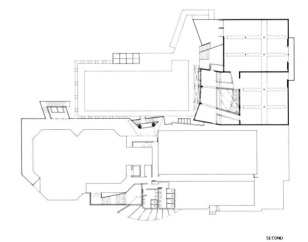

SECOND

Second floor plan

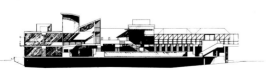

Section

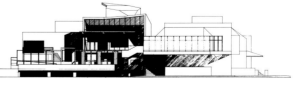

Elevation

GUTHRIE + BURESH

**SportCenter** Redondo Beach, California 1988-1989

An existing fitness facility in Redondo Beach was to undergo an extensive renovation and a 20,000 square foot addition, including new workout and locker rooms and a lap pool placed over a parking garage. The design works with a proposed 160-room hotel on an adjacent site to create a courtyard facing the ocean.

Plans

66

Composite perspective

Perspective from inside out looking towards exterior

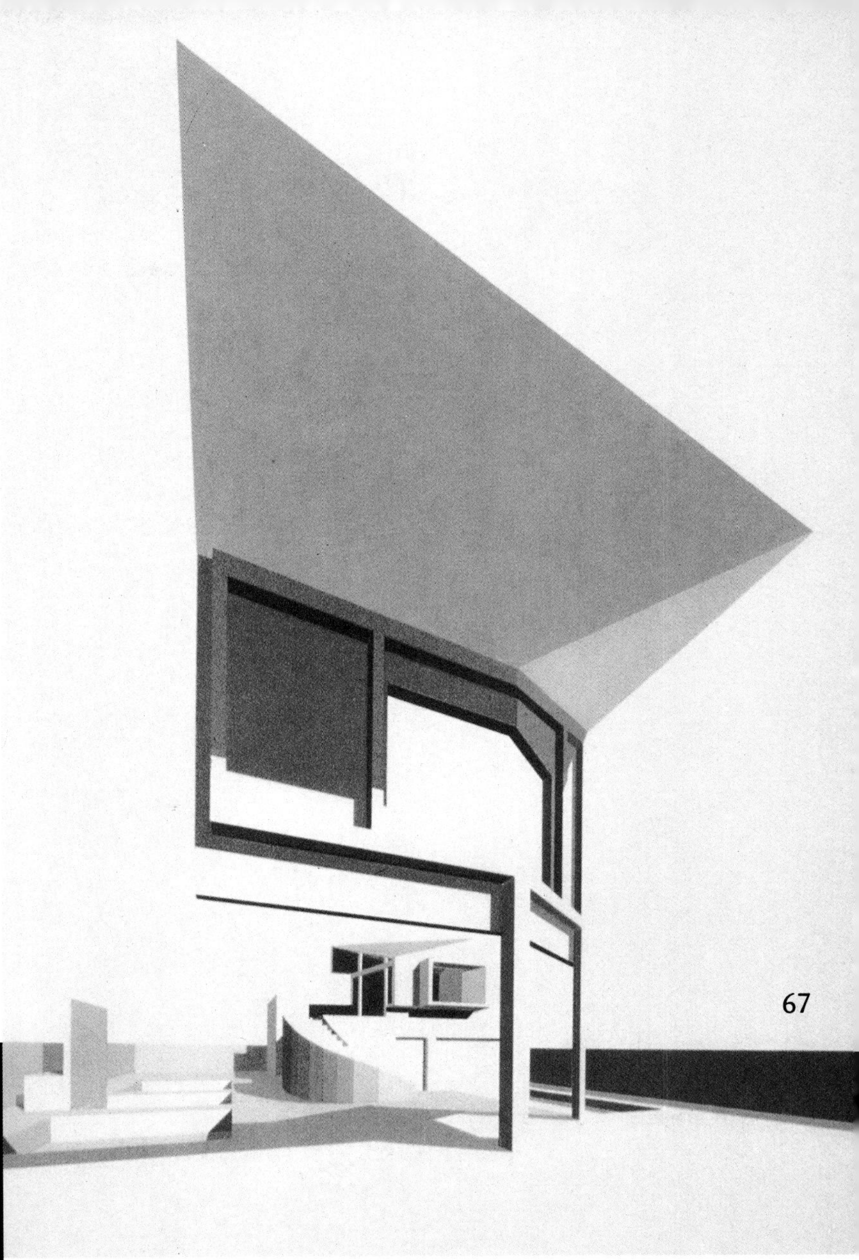

**550 Fortieth Street** San Pedro, California 1989-1990

This remodel and addition to a classic California bungalow in San Pedro consists of a narrow extension of the existing house into the garden and the placement of a garage and studio into a suburban backyard that has been transformed into an outdoor room.



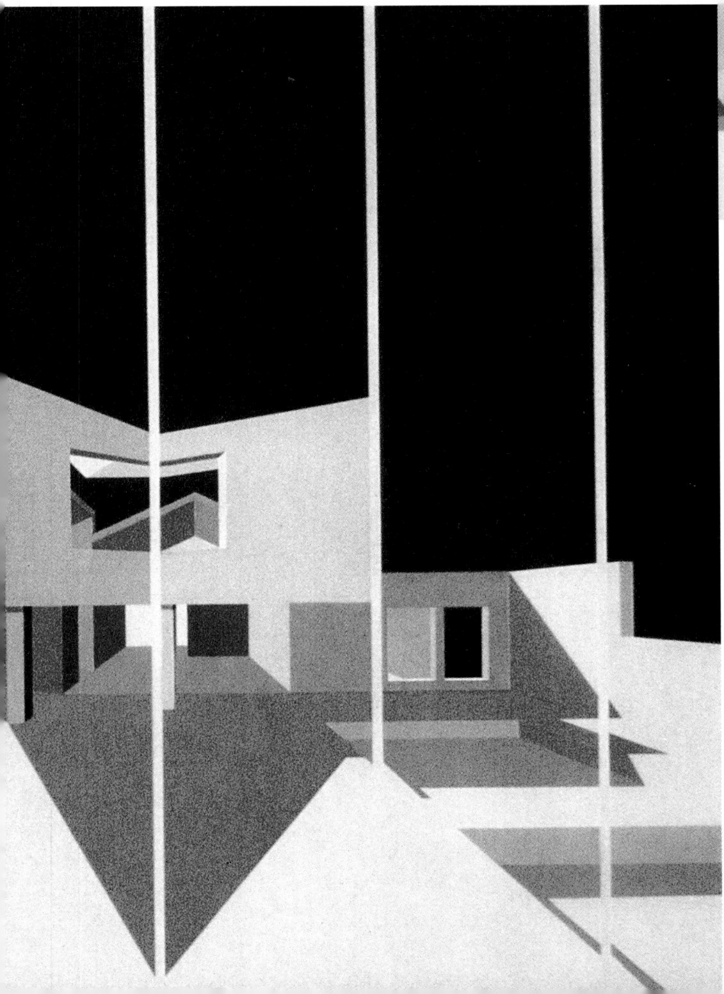

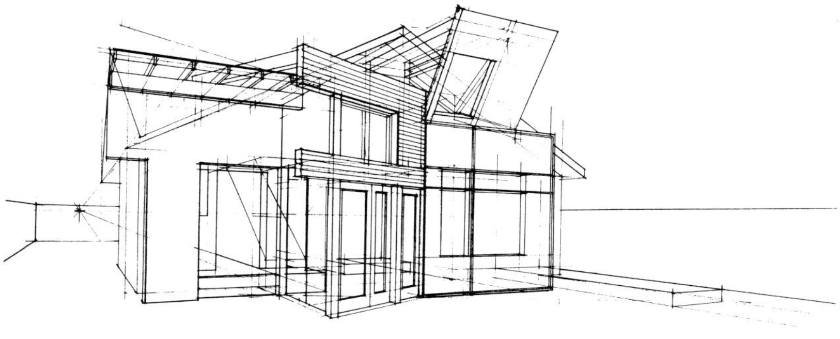

Perspective

**Frederick Kiesler Exhibit** Whitney Museum of American Art

New York, New York 1989

The design of the exhibition frames, in a series of modules, the wide range of styles and media in which Kiesler worked. The modules are meant to create an interactive environment rather than a neutral container.

**CHRISTIAN HUBERT**

Education:

Bachelor of Arts

Columbia University

Master of Architecture

Harvard University

Professional Experience:

CH Design

Richard Meier, Architects

**ANDIE ZELNIO**

Education:

Bachelor of Architecture

University of Arizona

Bachelor of Fine Arts

Western Illinois University

Professional Experience:

NBBJ/Larson, Architects

Frederick Fisher, Architect

# HUBERT/ZELNIO

68

**Mosquitos Shoe Store** Beverly Hills, California 1989

A 500-square-foot store designed for Mosquitos shoes. The primary materials are colored plaster walls, maple flooring, and steel display shelves. The transparent edge of this "shoebox" uses black aluminum and brick to frame views of the interior, while a steel and limestone display table projects through the glass storefront.

**Stewart Residence** Los Angeles, California 1988-1990

70

Originating from an existing house and an incomplete renovation, the
Stewart Residence project is assembled out of a series of discrete
architectural elements. Volumetric hinges, visual axes and layered
facades then are used to transform this assemblage of pavilions into a
unified collage.

71

Hall

**Walla/Sussman Apartment** New York, New York  1990

The Walla/Sussman Apartment integrates two separate units on different floors of a nineteenth-century federal-style row house characterized by elegant details but restricted spaces. A two-story greenhouse provides a link between the two parts of the house while expanding its programmatic and experimental scale. The interior surfaces and details play with the clients' interest in the contrast of the midcentury modern style with the historical detailing of the rest of the house.

In this multi-use project the surface of the street extends continuously through the loggia and into the interiors of the ground-floor shops and offices. The floors above are devoted to housing and offices, while the roof level has public terraces, restaurants, and an outdoor theater.

Perspective

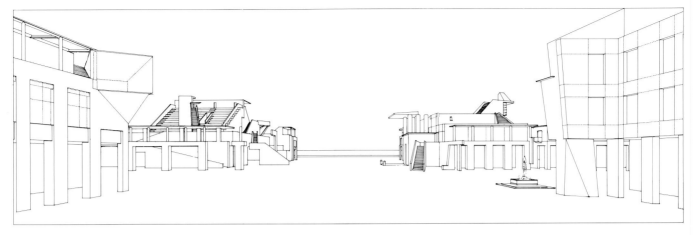

74

# JOHNSON FAVARO

**STEVEN JOHNSON**

Education:

Bachelor of Architecture
University of Florida at Gainesville, 1979
Master of Architecture
Graduate School of Design,
Harvard University, 1983

Professional Experience:

Koetter, Kim & Associates
Morphosis Architects

**JAMES FAVARO**

Education:

Bachelor of Science in Engineering
Stanford University, 1978
Master of Architecture
Graduate School of Design,
Harvard University, 1982

Professional Experience:

Machado/Silvetti Associates
Skidmore, Owings & Merrill

Interior perspective

**Yosemite West Hotel** Yosemite Valley, California 1990

A 500-room hotel, sited atop a high ridge in Yosemite National Park, appears to emerge from the granite outcroppings while nestled within an existing forest. The hotel is part of a master plan envisioning two hotels, 3,000 housing units and a large commercial center, all fitted into a steep site.

75

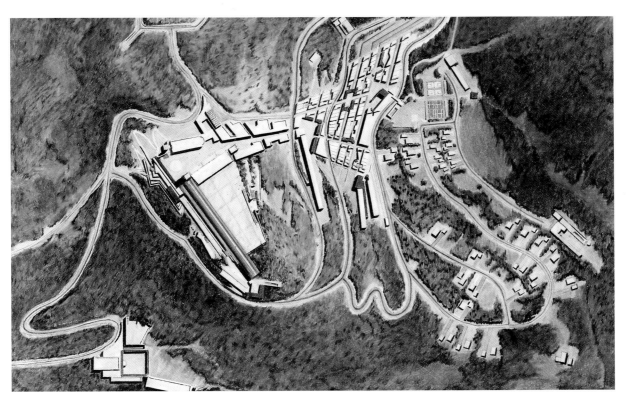

Plan

JOHNSON FAVARO

**DAVID KELLEN**

Education:

Bachelor of Arts (Mathematics)
UCLA, 1974
Master of Architecture,
UCLA Graduate School of Architecture
and Urban Planning, 1980

# DAVID KELLEN

Reception

Conference room

**Shalek Agency** Santa Monica, California 1989-1990

These offices for a Santa Monica advertising agency employ strong and simple forms finished in stucco. The vertical space is expanded at the ceiling plane by the removal of ceiling tiles and the painting of the grid and duct work above it in subtle colors.

THE SHALEK AGENCY

SUITE 400

NO SHOES SHIRT SERVICE

Entrance

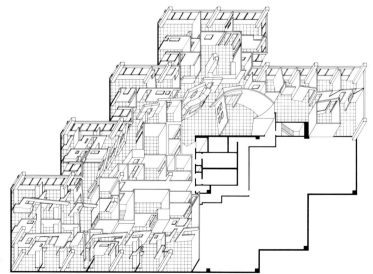

Axonometric

Model

78

**Children's Center for the Arts/Food Pavilion** Arts Park L.A. Competition
San Fernando Valley, California 1990

Organized around a nautilus shape, this project consists of a landscape of varied forms that invites children to
explore and discover. The project was also an experiment in collaboration and was designed with planner
Jefferson Eliot, landscape architects Land Studio and artist Judd Fine.

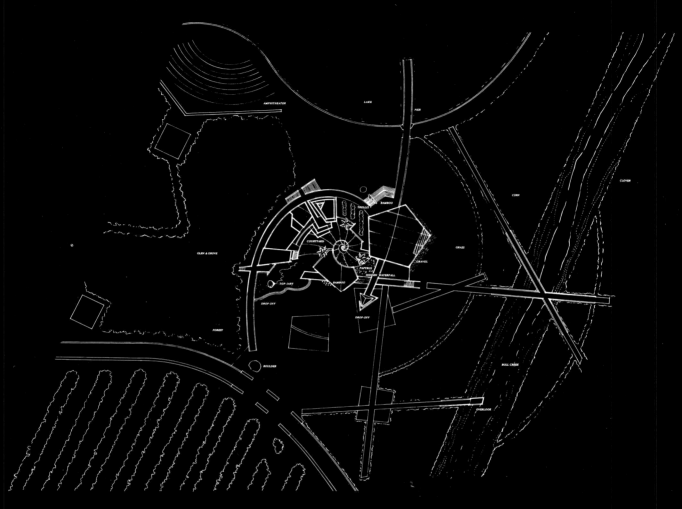

Plan

Section and elevations

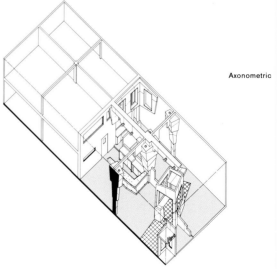

Axonometric

**Fama Restaurant** Santa Monica, California 1989

The dining room of this small restaurant is designed as an abstraction of an urban courtyard, containing sculptural forms that mimic those of the surrounding urban environment. The result is an expressionistic installation meant to be both challenging and playful.

83

# YOUNG ARCHITECTS IN LOS ANGELES. SOCIAL, POLITICAL AND CULTURAL CONTEXT.

By Leon Whiteson

In Los Angeles the private realm is particularly rich and varied, stocked with an array of houses, apartments, and gardens whose size and amenities New Yorkers, Londoners, or Tokyoites might envy. On the other hand, Los Angeles's public places, its few parks and plazas, are poor and neglected, and seem to be essentially marginal in the life of the huge regional metropolis that Southern California has become since World War II.

This extreme social imbalance between its private and public realms has long had a profound effect upon the character and range of architecture that characterizes Los Angeles. Put simply, Los Angeles's residential architecture is as remarkable as its public architecture, both civic and commercial, is generally dull and trashy. A casual visitor to the city with no access to the often-hidden houses that line its avenues or dot its hillsides would draw the conclusion from observing its nonresidential buildings that Los Angeles is either considerably less affluent than its Hollywood mythology has led the world to believe, or else it simply does not care what public face it shows.

In the century since Los Angeles has evolved from a sleepy pueblo to a major metropolis, almost all its best architectural talents have put most of their energies into designing houses. In fact, from the era of the "craftsman" masterpieces by Charles and Henry Greene and the California bungalow the craftsman style popularized, Southern California has given the nation and the world an innovative domestic architecture, including the mission style, the Spanish colonial revival style, the protomodernism of Irving Gill, the early California modernism of Rudolph Schindler and Richard Neutra, the 1930s streamline moderne style, the post–World War II Case Study Houses engendered by *Arts & Architecture* editor, John Entenza, the ranch house developed mainly by Cliff May, and on up to Frank Gehry's much-admired pop-modernism.

Gehry's experience in Los Angeles graphically illustrates the private-public imbalance. Only recently has Gehry been commissioned to design a major public building in his hometown, the new Disney Concert Hall on Bunker Hill. His other public buildings here—the Loyola Law School campus, the Hollywood Library, and the Space Museum in Exposition Park—are either only semipublic or small in scale. Morphosis, one of the leaders of the post-Gehry generation, has been limited to the creation of several trendy restaurants and a largely hidden underground cancer treatment center at Cedars Sinai Hospital.

A look at the work of the young designers included in this book reveals that this overwhelmingly residential trend continues hot and strong. Given that most young architects anywhere in the United States cut their professional teeth on the design of houses, or additions to houses, in Los Angeles many architects may do few nonresidential projects for most of their careers.

Yet, in the private realm, the local history of enlightened patronage has given Los Angeles's domestic designers the freedom to experiment and innovate. From Frank Lloyd Wright's client Aline

Barnsdall on to the Lovells, who commissioned land-mark houses from both Schindler and Neutra in the 1930s, to patrons such as the Cuthbertsons, who gave Eric Owen Moss an early opportunity to explore his obsessions with the process of reconstruction in an unstable urban environment, house-building Angelenos have been willing to take chances with new and unusual talents.

Though "unencumbered by taste," as the local novelist Aviva Layton characterizes the Los Angeles clientele, individual Angelenos have long had the moxie to go way out on a stylistic limb. The Mayan-inspired textile-block houses Frank Lloyd Wright designed in Hollywood in the 1920s were, and still are, unlike anything seen anywhere, locally or nationally. Eric Owen Moss's gull-winged Petal House and Frank Gehry's famous or, according to his immediate neighbors, notorious, chain-link-shrouded Santa Monica house have become quintessentially Angeleno icons.

And the tradition of innovative patronage continues strongly. Norman Millar's Hedge House, John Chase's Magistrale Bungalow, O'Herlihy + Warner's O'Herlihy House, Hubert/Zelnio's Stewart Residence, Josh Schweitzer's desert house, houses by Janek Bielski and Koning Eizenberg, and Guthrie + Buresh's "exploded bungalow" have all found clients willing to allow emerging talents to explore new forms or reenergize old ones.

While Norman Millar might describe his architecture as a "quest for appropriateness, economy and delight," or O'Herlihy + Warner talk of a search for "an architectural order which embraces the elemental language of construction," most young talents are simply flexing their aesthetic muscles.

Nonresidential projects that have also given designers license to experiment and invent include restaurants, shops, and independent film and TV production houses. These projects allow architects to make a showing in the public realm, if only to a limited degree.

Following the lead of Morphosis's Angeli, 72 Market, and Kate Mantilini eateries and Gehry's Rebecca, Schweitzer and Kellen have created City Restaurant, Kellen designed Fama, Schweitzer did Border Grill 2, and Michele Saee has designed Trattoria Angeli.

The Hollywood category of independent film and TV production houses has opened another area to architectural expression. Following Frank Israel's designs for Propaganda Films and his revamping of the old Charles and Ray Eames studio in Venice, Victoria Casasco has designed a studio for Darymple Productions and Blake + Au have created remarkably vivid scenarios for Red Dog Films and Mambo Films. The young designers declare that "the most pervasive influence [is] the city of Los Angeles itself, with its layers of idio-syncratic ideas."

These "layers of idiosyncratic ideas" seem to be rooted, for most of the emerging generation, in the vibrant, often trashy populism of Los Angeles. In fact, a species of high-minded populism has come to be the Angeleno trademark since Gehry came to prominence in the late 1970s.

This Angeleno populism, epitomized in the "Googie" architecture of the 1950s coffee shops such as Ship's and Norm's, and such beloved popular icons as the hotdog-shaped Tail O' the Pup fastfood stand, is a vital source of creative renewal for young local designers.

Bielski talks of "formal issues which comment on the disjointed pop culture" in a "collage city" in which "emerging rituals and mythologies . . . integrate and give meaning to our predicaments." Bielski, in his one major public project, a prize-winning entry for the West Hollywood Civic Center, gives expression to a tension between "the need for intimacy and the scale of the auto."

In a reference to the insecurity many Angelenos feel about the physical nature of their built environment, Michele Saee suggests that "we have lost our relationship with the spaces we live in. . . [which] adds to our awareness of the changeable nature of the world around us." AKS Runo, one of the firms most concerned with the public realm, states that Los Angeles's architectural space "outstrips the rationality of the European eye [in] the simultaneous occurrence of multitudes of things." The Central Office of Architecture declares that "No longer is the total theater of the contemporary city explicable as a series of related events," and Ron McCoy, while designing a beachfront house, worries about the way his walls have to "jump, bend and break to express the conflicting pressures of the inside and the outside."

Such statements reveal that young designers, like an increasing number of Los Angeles residents, feel the heightened pressures of the public realm beyond the boundaries of their private spaces. They are beginning to share an understanding, forced upon a tradition of Angeleno individuality, that the gang markers of Latino Boyle Heights are directly connected to the "Armed Response" signs that dot the lawns of affluent Bel Air.

These pressures spring from several sources. One is the fact that the County of Los Angeles, which counts eighty-six cities and nine million people within its boundaries, has run out of space for urban expansion to accommodate the thousands of new residents drawn to the region's vigorous and expansive economy. This pressure has led to a strong popular reaction against the traffic congestion caused by commercial and residential development, especially in the more privileged areas, such as the Westside and the northern slopes of the Santa Monica Mountains in the San Fernando Valley.

Another pressure comes from the rapid change in the area's demographics. In the past ten years, Los Angeles's population has gone from a majority of Anglos to a polyglot populace in which Latinos, Asians, and African-Americans outnumber the Anglos. As a sign of the times, the Los Angeles Unified School District is now eighty-five percent nonwhite in its enrollment. Hollywood High School, which once educated the children of film stars, now counts more than eighty different languages native to its students.

A result of these pressures is the ghettoization of the city as the largely white "haves" seek to insulate themselves from the unfamiliar "have-nots." A great deal of the antigrowth sentiment rampant in Los Angeles is fed by the urge to keep white enclaves free of blacks, browns, and yellows. "No-growthers are often racist," says former Los Angeles City Planning Commission president Daniel Garcia with typical bluntness.

But the restless and underprivileged nonwhites won't stay put. Gang members have taken to prowling previously safe white areas such as Marina del Rey and Westwood, making McCoy's walls "jump, bend and break." The notorious Latino and black Oakwood ghetto borders beachfront Venice, where so many innovative architects have designed houses and restaurants. Herds of bedraggled homeless people haunt the neat oceanfront promenade of Santa Monica, where many designers live and have their offices. "We live in a changing world of ethnic diversity and technological innovation accompanied by crumbling infrastructures," says RAW Architecture's Roland Wiley. "In such an environment, what is the character of 'pure design?'"

In the midst of this cultural tension and confusion, "pure design" is simultaneously an escape from harsh realities and a way out of a situation over which the individual has little control.

Michael Burch talks of his "interest in elemental forms and materials . . . [in an] attempt to achieve richness and tension through the simplest of means." Chase, on the other hand, looks back to the California bungalow, which he describes as "rustic but genteel," in a sentimental nostalgia for an imagined "pure" past when Los Angeles was the dreamed-of haven of migrating middle America. And Schweitzer says, "I strive for 'stillness' through simplicity."

Schweitzer's designs demonstrate a desire to express a flavor of Los Angeles's increasing ethnic diversity, especially the historic presence of its Latino community, without sentimentality. Eschewing any parody of the region's Spanish colonial revival tradition, Schweitzer's Desert House Monument in the Joshua Tree National Monument area are, in their strong and simple planes and vivid colors, influenced by the work of Mexican architects Luis Barragan and Ricardo Legorreta.

Apart from this direct aesthetic derivation, there is, as yet, little evidence that non-Anglo traditions have had much effect on the styles preferred by the younger generation. There is, for instance, no equivalent in Southern California of the "tropical" modernism developed in Miami by Arquitectonica. The local influences here remain overwhelmingly Eurocentric, filtered through mainstream American populism feeding into the sunny California imagery evoked by Hollywood.

Perhaps this clinging to tradition—not something many observers note about Southern California—comes from the volatile and essentially unsettled nature of Angeleno life.

In *Southern California: An Island in the Land*, Carey McWilliams quotes a visitor's comment that "the whole population is immigrant, with the slowly changing sense of home peculiar to non-indigenous life . . . [so that] for a long time there will be in the cells a memory of home that was elsewhere." Put simply, Southern California is a society of strangers in which the common ground is precious in its very tenuousness. This is the country of the mind where it is vital to wish "Have a nice day" to every new face, to establish some sort of mutuality.

At the same time, almost all the buildings one sees in Los Angeles were the very first structures ever to appear on their lots. Los Angeles is a first-growth metropolis that is beginning to run out of vacant land.

A number of the projects that engage young architects are exercises in laying down a second growth upon the first. Sometimes this is literally so, as in Burch's design for the expansion of Jonathan Martin Inc., in which he considers a "set of individual forms. . .playing off against the mass of the existing brick building." Wagner + Webb's Santa Monica Stone Garden "sows seeds in the urban fabric," they say, though that fabric may be very loosely woven in Los Angeles. Koning Eizenberg try to build the city's volatility into their architecture by creating "buildings that can take change."

The perception that Angeleno life is seldom static or "finished," and that its architecture cannot easily attain the completeness of more settled societies, was one of Frank Gehry's great insights. This is an ad hoc culture in which people and institutions make themselves up as they go along, and always seem aware that a changeable tomorrow is already here. For this reason, Los Angeles architecture is often makeshift to the point of trashiness, a series of strip facades in which the shop signs and the monster billboards that hover over them are more assertive than the buildings they advertise.

Projects such as Norman Millar's Almor liquor store play off against the sign-dominated strip-trash idiom by making much of its own upfront scenography, which shows no pretense of being more than two-dimensional. The Central Office of Architecture contrives a vivid facadism for the Brix Restaurant in Venice as a response to the "chaotic commercial character of the context." In fact, the very trashiness of streets such as Melrose Avenue has allowed the district's swift and lively transformation from a typical commercial strip into an urban movie set in which upscale young Angelenos posture and parade. All it took was a change in the style of shop names, a lick of fresh paint, an evocative detail or two, a quick design gesture here and there, and *voila!* — instant theater.

Apart from such small-scale designs, the vigorous and inventive architecture that wells up from the younger generation has had little impact on the style of most of the civic and commercial structures being built today. Most new office buildings, shopping centers, and apartment complexes in Los Angeles follow the bland modernist or watered-down postmodernist idioms seen in every U.S. city. Los Angeles's more innovative designers are effectively shut out of the power structure that finances such large-scale, mainstream projects, and in that sense they remain peripheral to the life of the city.

There's nothing new about this. Schindler, Neutra, Gill, the Case Study House designers, and on up to Gehry were seldom given a shot at major public projects. Gehry, typically, had to make an international reputation before he was awarded the Disney Hall complex in 1988, and even then he had to compete for it with the likes of Britain's James Stirling, Germany's Gottfried Boehm, and Austria's Hans Hollein. Even today, Gehry is considered a "wild man" by most mainstream Angelenos, and the younger designers he influenced, known collectively as The Gehry Kids, remain essentially marginal in Los Angeles, despite their reputation elsewhere in the United States and the world.

Though operating on the margin, The Gehry Kids, particularly that first generation of now-aging experimentalists that lie between the master and the designers in this book, have discovered enough adventurous hometown patrons to be able to survive professionally, if often precariously. This gallery of talents — including Morphosis, Frank Israel, Craig Hodgetts, Robert Mangurian, Eric Owen Moss, Fred Fisher, and others — has developed a small local clientele willing to explore variations and elaborations of Gehryian pop-modernism.

In Los Angeles, however, marginality does not imply irrelevance. On the contrary, this is a cultural environment in which the margin is often central. Lacking a sense of being centered, Los Angeles's style is frequently set by a few gifted people working on the periphery.

Hollywood is a classic case. In its heyday between the two World Wars, the movie industry was always economically, socially, and culturally marginal to the Angeleno mainstream. Self-obsessed with its role as dream factory to the world, Hollywood made a showy splash that showered little upon most of Los Angeles's populace. Now that it has become merely another business controlled by giant corporations headquartered in New York or Tokyo, Hollywood's once-marginal-yet-vital creativity has been taken over by its offspring — MTV. Developed by such small outfits as Propaganda Films, MTV has assumed the film and TV industry's trend-creating role for a new generation.

Another famous instance of the power of the periphery in Los Angeles is that of Charles and Ray Eames' Pacific Palisades house. An icon of what came to be known as high-tech, the Eames House has inspired designers in many countries, yet never gave birth to a local style. And then there is Watts Towers, the masterfully intuitive creation of the untutored and lonely Italian immigrant Sabatino Rodia in the trough of the Los Angeles Basin. A unique act of visionary architecture, Watts Towers haunts the edges of every Angeleno designer's consciousness as a symbol of the imaginative power of a solitary soul.

It is remarkable that Los Angeles's vaunted climate of creative freedom manages to cohabit with a stubborn cultural indifference — nay, philistinism — in the region. The city is a weird mixture of innovation and ignorance, of the whacko and the who-cares? That culturally first-rate and fifth-rate strains mingle without restraint is epitomized in the region's major newspaper, *The Los Angeles Times*, whose columns can be both remarkably sophisticated and unashamedly redneck on the same page.

Major institutions that have the power to confer cultural cachet are, with the completion of Arata Isozaki's Museum of Contemporary Art and the promise of Gehry's Disney Hall and Richard Meier's Getty Center, only just beginning to create a presence on the city's profile. With no major art, architecture, or literary publications based in California, the machinery for making a national reputation does not yet exist on the West Coast, despite the region's artistic and economic vitality and prominence.

Many designers applaud this absence of cultural infrastructures. They like the lack of institutions and publications and the rarity of any first-rate critical commentary, which they feel leaves them free to experiment and innovate without constantly having to look over their shoulders for instant evaluation. However, the situation leaves Los Angeles vulnerable to the kind of cultural carpetbagging in which East Coast mandarins seize upon preconceived manifestations of "Californication," and thereby perpetuate self-fulfilling prophecies about the region's flakiness.

For all its fertile confusions, engaging shallowness, bland barbarities, and shameless self-love, Southern California remains one of the most interesting places for a young architect to practice.

Los Angeles artlessly reveals the tensions of a polyglot regional metropolis in the intensely fluid Information Age. Yet, the city constantly generates the human resources needed to match these often-terrifying challenges.

The young designers whose work appears in this book demonstrate a boldness and talent to conjure a vital response to such challenges, creating an increasingly urban and urbane imagery to mirror Los Angeles's slippery soul.

View from street

# KONING EIZENBERG

**HANK KONING**

Education:

Bachelor of Architecture
Melbourne University, 1977
Master of Architecture
UCLA Graduate School of Architecture
and Urban Planning, 1981

Professional Experience:

Hank Romyn, Architect, Melbourne
Max May, Architect, Melbourne
UCLA Urban Innovations Group

**JULIE EIZENBERG**

Education:

Bachelor of Architecture
Melbourne University, 1977
Master of Architecture
UCLA Graduate School of Architecture
and Urban Planning, 1981

Professional Experience:

Jackson & Walker, Architects, Melbourne
Public Works Dept., Victoria
Max May, Architect, Melbourne

**Hollywood Duplex**
Hollywood, California 1987

Two single-family homes on a steeply sloped lot in the Hollywood Hills are placed on either side of a narrow passage that fans out to private terraces on the hillside in the back of the lot, while maintaing a visual connection from the street to the hillside.

91

View from rear

View from street

**Berkeley Street Project** Santa Monica, California 1988

The City of Santa Monica and a local hospital jointly developed this program for low-income, subsidized rental housing. The design creates seven 2- and 3-bedroom units over a parking area in a largely residential neighborhood, drawing on the Southern California version of modernism in a socially inclusive way.

Front facade

**Ken Edwards Center** Santa Monica California 1990

The Ken Edwards Center attempts to create a non-institutional setting for the senior citizens who occupy it by dividing the facility into a village-like grouping of buildings centered on a courtyard.

93

Courtyard

View of studio and living room from rear

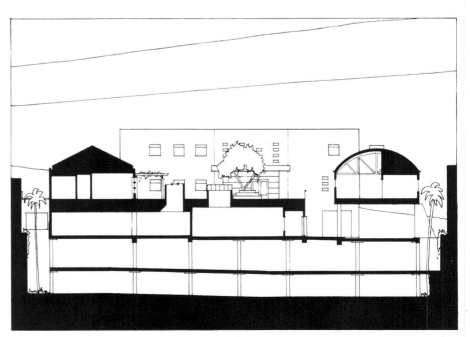

**6th Street Project** Santa Monica, California 1988

Like the Berkeley Street Project, these rental units attempt to create a strong internal identity while mediating between the variety of scale of the surrounding residential neighborhood of Santa Monica. They consist of six 1- to 4-bedroom rental apartments (two reserved for senior citizens) over a parking area.

**Koning Eizenberg House** Santa Monica, California 1989

The architects' design for their own home sits on a narrow lot shared with two small bungalows. A two-story studio and living-room block is connected to the main body of the house by a glass-enclosed bridge.

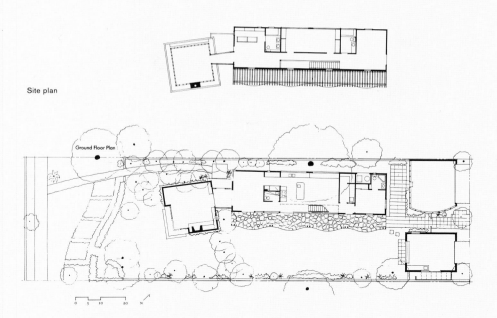

Site plan

Ground Floor Plan

0  5  10      20      N

View from street

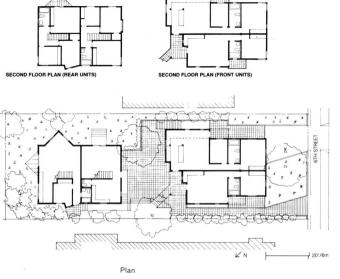

SECOND FLOOR PLAN (REAR UNITS)        SECOND FLOOR PLAN (FRONT UNITS)

Plan

N        20'/6m

KONING EIZENBERG

**Krane/Kellerman Residence Addition**  Hollywood Hills, California  1989

This project consists of a series of additions to an earlier addition by Frank Gehry for the hillside home of an actress and a film executive. The clearly defined forms are intended to contrast with both earlier structures.

96

# LUBOWICKI LANIER

**PAUL LUBOWICKI**

Education:

Bachelor of Architecture
The Cooper Union, 1977

Professional Experience:

Frank O. Gehry & Associates
Richard Serra (Collaboration)
Claes Oldenburg (Collaboration)
Anthony Caro (Collaboration)

**SUSAN LANIER**

Education:

Bachelor of Arts in Psychology
Pitzer College, 1971
Master of Architecture
Southern California Institute
of Architecture, 1988

Professional Experience:

Morphosis Architects

Bales of raw material

Bale Chair #1

**Bale Chair** #1  1988-1989

The Bale Chair is a project for a prototype line of furniture using recycled shredded paper that is baled like hay after it has been shredded.  This chair is made from shredded telephone books carved out with a chain saw and includes a stereo hidden within the bale.

Model

**O'Neill Guest House**

West Los Angeles, California  1988-1990

The design of this house was inspired by the Crazy Cat cartoons of George Herriman. The home is assembled from a group of discrete, yet expressive, elements.

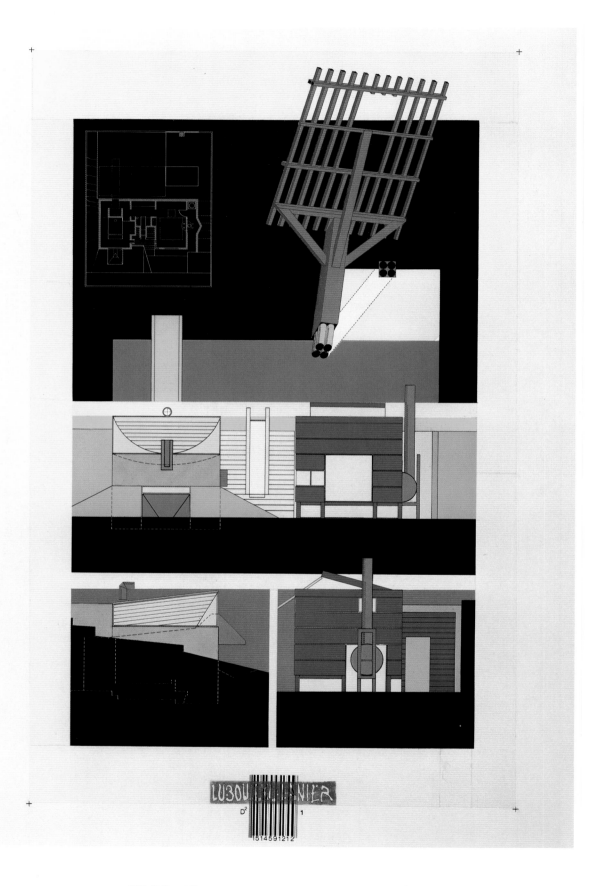

98

**O'Neill Guest House**   Sections

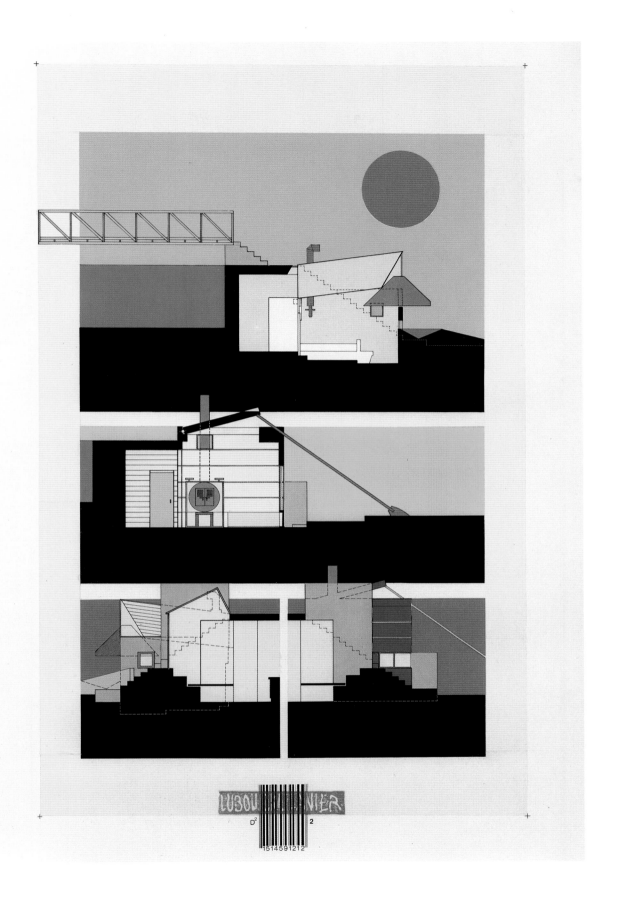

# OFFICE OF CHARLES AND ELIZABETH LEE

**UCLA Childcare Center** Los Angeles, California   1988

The buildings for the Childcare Center were prefabricated off site to facilitate a short construction schedule. The buildings are transparent and enhance the children's environment through the use of borrowed landscape.

## CHARLES DWIGHT LEE

Education:

Bachelor of Science in Architecture
University of Southern California, 1974
Master of Architecture
University of Southern California, 1976

Professional Experience:

Foster Associates Inc., Hong Kong
Bobrow Thomas & Associates
William Periera and Associates
Albert C. Martin & Associates
Archisystems
Studio di Urbanistica et Architettura, Milan

## ELIZABETH LI-SHING WANG LEE

Education:

Bachelor of Architecture
University of Southern California, 1984

Professional Experience:

Foster Associates Inc., Hong Kong
Bobrow Thomas & Associates
William Periera and Associates
Charles Kober & Associates
Konrad Wachsmann, USC

101

Hall

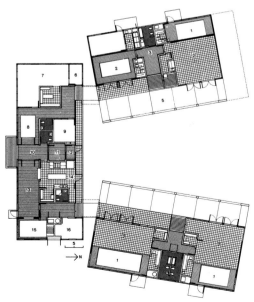

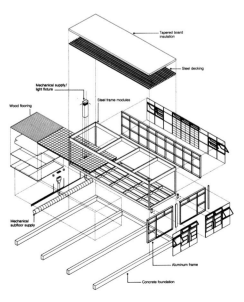

**UCLA Children's Center**   Plan   Isometric

103

Classroom

Entry

**Northwest Campus Recreation
Center Tennis Stadium**
UCLA Campus, Los Angeles 1990

A new stadium complex for the UCLA campus consists of grandstand seating for 500 spectators, support facilities for 10 new tennis courts, an office building, and a parking structure for 150 cars. The tennis courts are terraced for a minimal impact on the landscape.

Elevation

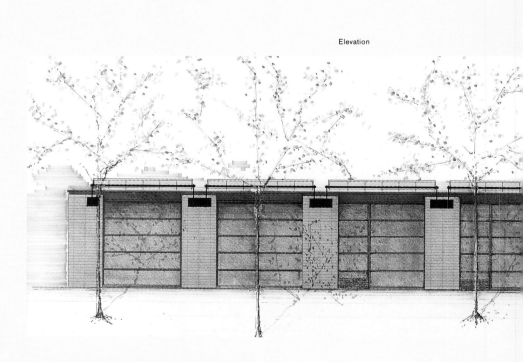

**Broadway-Spring Center** Los Angeles, California 1991

The Broadway-Spring Center combines the features of a park and a small, 5,000-square-foot retail center.
The three retail buildings are sited like pavilions in a garden.

Section

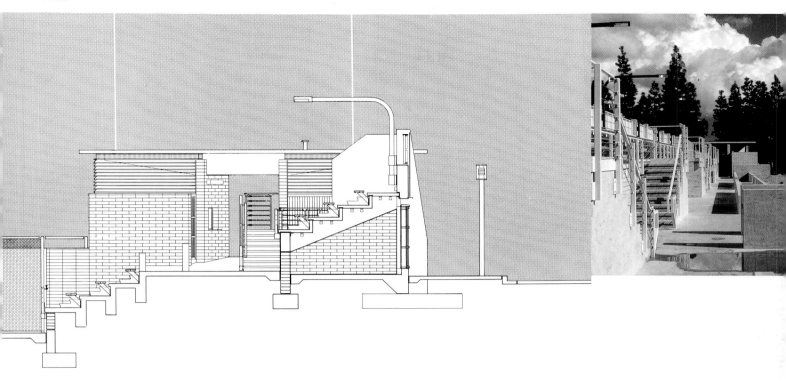

105

Sign

Detail

CHARLES & ELIZABETH LEE

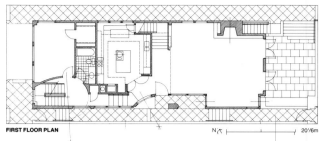

**FIRST FLOOR PLAN**

N↑ ⊢———————⊣ 20'/6m

# RON McCOY

106

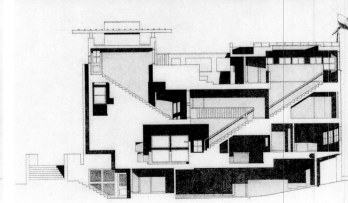

**RON MC COY**

Education:

Bachelor of Architecture
University of Southern California, 1978
Master of Architecture
Princeton University, 1980

Professional Experience:

Michael Graves, Architect
Venturi, Scott Brown & Associates

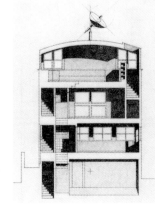

Cross section

Longitudinal section

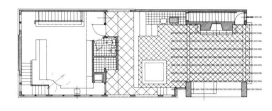

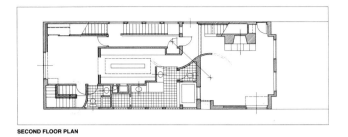

**SECOND FLOOR PLAN**

Roof deck

107

Front facade

RON MC COY

**Webb Residence** Marina del Rey, California 1988-1990

A detached single-family home with distant views of the ocean is organized as a series of vertically layered spaces, discrete and formal, that culminate in an open roof deck. The home's severe form addresses both the surrounding context and recent architectural excesses in the region.

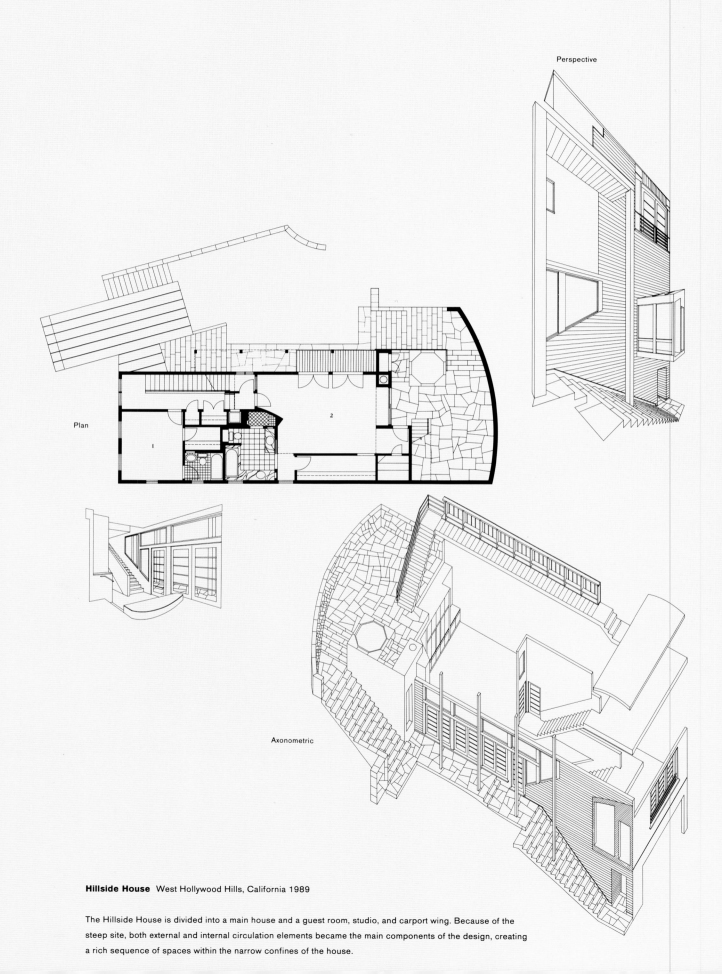

Perspective

Plan

Axonometric

**Hillside House** West Hollywood Hills, California 1989

The Hillside House is divided into a main house and a guest room, studio, and carport wing. Because of the
steep site, both external and internal circulation elements became the main components of the design, creating
a rich sequence of spaces within the narrow confines of the house.

**Grossman Residence**
Los Angeles, California
1986-1987

The Grossman Residence addition consists of a small breakfast room and the renovation of an existing kitchen. The cabinets are made of rift-sawn ash with a deep green stain. The handle is a composite panel of solid ash with a stainless steel pull and a rosewood spine.

109

Detail of cabinetry

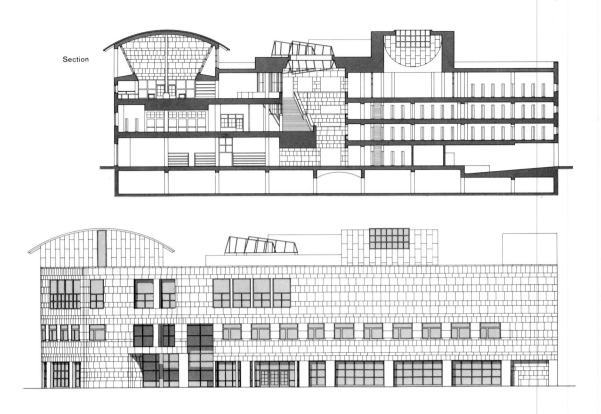

Section

**Evanston Public Library**
**Competition Entry**
Evanston, Illinois 1991

The Evanston Public Library is designed as a relatively solid and deliberate building on a significant public corner in the center of the city, near the Northwestern University campus. The regularity of the limestone walls is emphasized by the ground level rhythm of storefront windows. Two dominant exceptions are the eroded corner entry loggia, accentuated by a plaza paved with the atlas of the world, and the large vaulted space of the reference room at the third level.

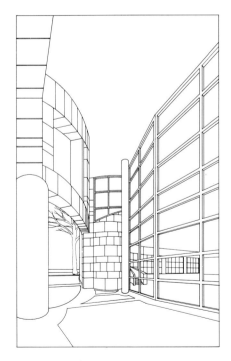

Entry loggia

Stairwell perspective

Interior perspective, reference room

Perspective

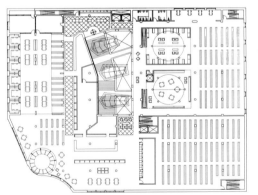

Third floor plan

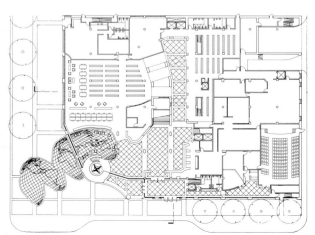

First floor plan

**NORMAN MILLAR**

Education:

Bachelor of Arts

University of Washington, 1976

Master of Architecture

University of Pennsylvania, 1978

Professional Experience:

A2Z Partnership

Olson Walker, Architects

Baumgardner Architects

Model

# NORMAN MILLAR

Section

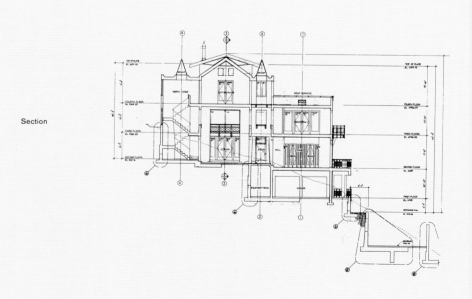

**Pentaplex House** Seattle, Washington 1990

The Pentaplex House, a five-unit apartment building, is located in Seattle's Broadway district. Sited on a 30 x 120-foot lot, its three towers are clad in galvanized corrugated metal and wood, and are ornamented with metalwork by artist Ries Niemi.

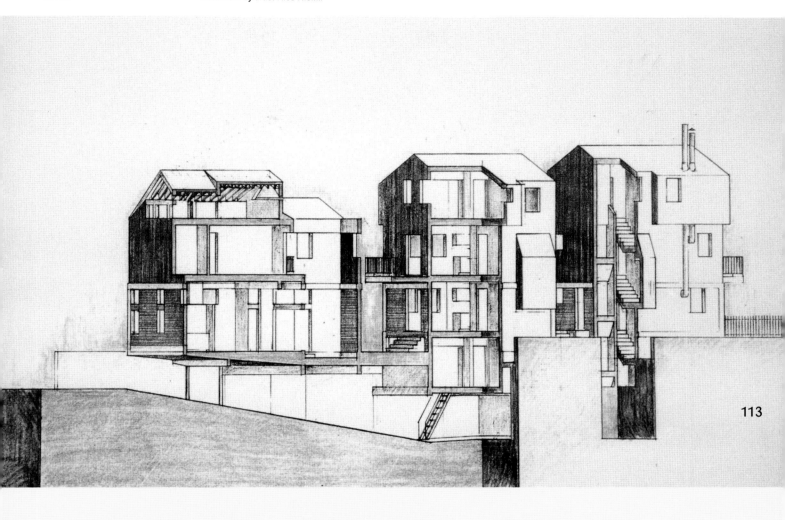

113

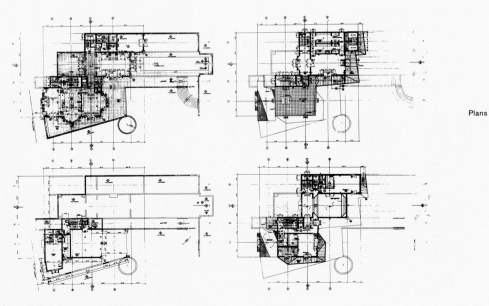

Plans

**Slide House** Los Angeles, California 1990

This 5000-square-foot house will be located in the Pacific Palisades overlooking the Pacific Ocean on a steep hill prone to landslides. The four-story house is designed to elude the worst slide areas and to give every room an ocean view.

NORMAN MILLAR

Front

## Almor Liquor Store Hollywood, California 1989

The street facade of the Almor Liquor store incorporates and critiques the spirit of the commercial vernacular storefront by elaborating on existing signage and transforming the small building into a collage of plaster, sheet metal and neon elements. The custom metal work was created by Gale McCall.

View from street

Rear

115

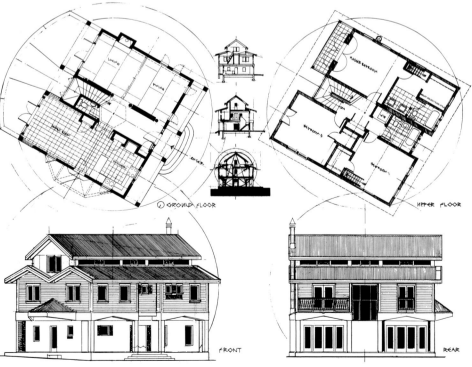

① GROUND FLOOR

UPPER FLOOR

FRONT

REAR

Plan/Elevation/Section

## Hedge House Los Angeles, California 1988

This three-bedroom house is located in Culver City, a Los Angeles neighborhood which consists predominantly of single-story, 1950s tract houses. The home's idiosyncratic site is surrounded by tall hedges that create the sensation of outdoor rooms.

**LORCAN O' HERLIHY**

Education:

Bachelor of Architecture
California Polytechnic State University
San Luis Obispo, 1981

Professional Experience:

Steven Holl, Architects
I.M.Pei & Partners
Kevin Roche John Dinkeloo & Associates

# O'HERLIHY + WARNER

**RICHARD WARNER**

Education:

Bachelor of Architecture
California Polytechnic State University
San Luis Obispo, 1981

Professional Experience:

Richard Warner, Architect
Steven Holl, Architects
Hellmuth, Obata & Kassabaum

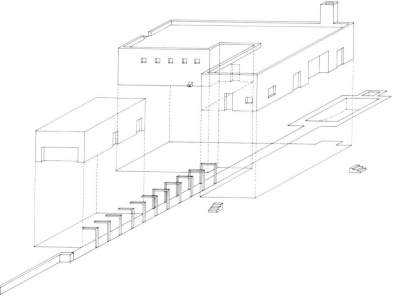

Isometric

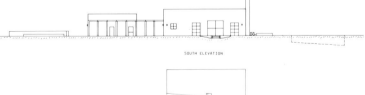

SOUTH ELEVATION

VIEW INTO COURTYARD

VIEW LOOKING EAST

**O'Herlihy House** Malibu, California 1987

Elevation and design sketches

The relationship of this house to its context is expressed metaphorically through the organization of its two major axes—one oriented toward the canyon, the other to the ocean. The home's unadorned white volumes deliberately contrast with the landscape.

118

**Freund-Koopman Residence** Pacific Palisades, California  1990

Interior perspective

This house addition and renovation attempts to create an ensemble of living volumes which engage the natural virtues of the site. The existing, inward-oriented house is oblivious to its beautiful wooded site on an ancient alluvial bluff in the Santa Monica Mountains.

119

Exterior perspective

Exterior perspective

Exterior perspectives

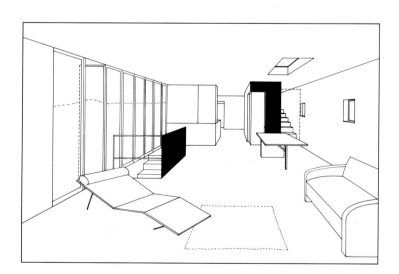

Interior perspective

**Lucey-Vanous Residence** Venice, California 1991

The site of the Lucey Residence contains two existing houses. The entire volume of the new house sits atop one of those homes, pushed up against the north side of the site and allowing for a swath of garden space along the south side.

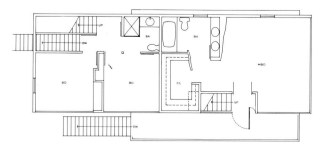

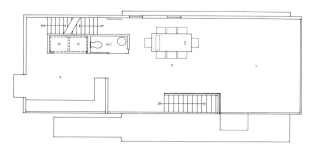

Plans

121

O'HERLIHY + WARNER

**Bernard Residence** Malibu, California 1991-1992

The Bernard House is a 5,800-square-foot house set on a hillside overlooking the Pacific Ocean.
The steel-trowelled plaster walls that make up the body of the building are punctuated by delicate steel
canopies and steel casement windows.

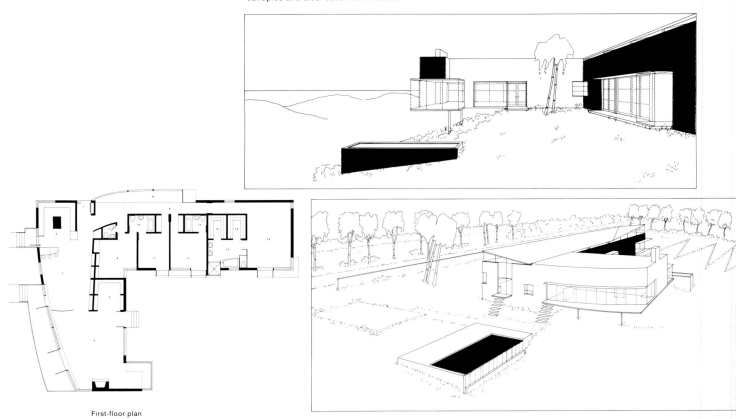

First-floor plan

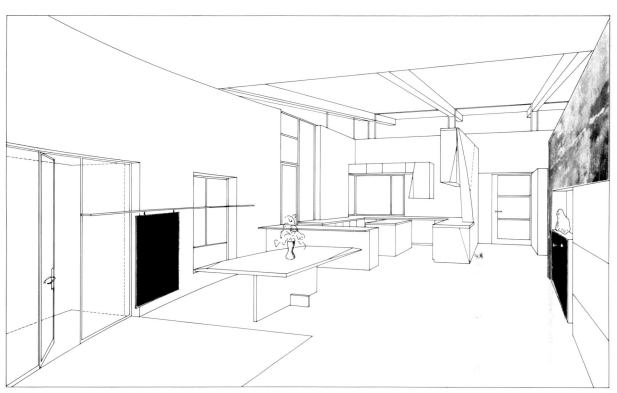

Interior perspective

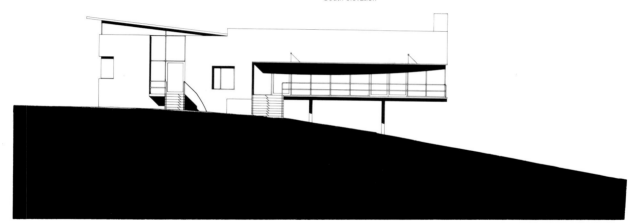

Model

123

# GARY PAIGE

**GARY PAIGE**

Education:

Bachelor of Architecture
Southern California Institute of
Architecture, 1980

**Arcana Bookstore** Santa Monica, California  1987

The remodeling of the Arcana Bookstore on the Santa Monica Mall involved the design and construction of new bookshelves and the refitting of the store's central space.

Design drawings

125

GARY PAIGE

126

**Akido Studio** Santa Monica, California 1991

The renovation of this martial arts studio is based on the principles of spherical rotation and lightness that form the basis of akido. This representation is achieved by leading the eye through an elliptical movement around a simple space where the ceiling has been shaped and windows have been manipulated to explore the different ways in which light can mold space.

**Sci-ARC Wall** Santa Monica, California   1989

Located in the main space of the Southern California Institute of Architecture, this wall construction was
intended as the first phase of a three-part remodeling of the building  The simple walls were meant to contrast
with the existing steel structure. The wall is layered and cut to convey a sense of massiveness.

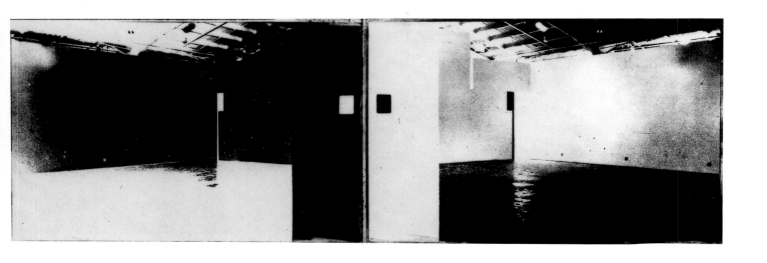

127

AND
THEY

DISSOLVED

LIKE

SHADOWS

Entrance

# RAW ARCHITECTURE

**R. STEVEN LEWIS**

Education:

Bachelor of Architecture and Urban Planning
Syracuse University

Professional Experience:

Gruen & Associates

**STEVEN G. LOTT**

Education:

Bachelor of Environmental Design
California State University at Pomona

**ROLAND A. WILEY**

Education:

Bachelor of Architecture
Ball State University, Indiana

Professional Experience:

Gruen & Associates

Interior hallway

Axonometric

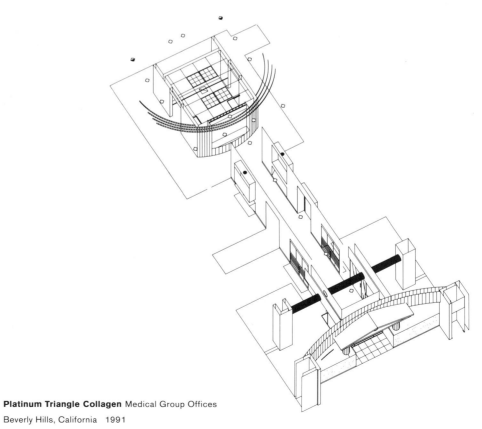

**Platinum Triangle Collagen** Medical Group Offices
Beverly Hills, California   1991

The interior of the offices is designed to function as an art gallery as well as a medical facility containing office spaces for waiting, examination, and consultation.  A formal geometry helps organize the extremely complex programs.

# MODERNISM AND THE

By John Chase

# LOS ANGELES VERNACULAR

As with any group of twenty-three architectural firms from one geographic area, these firms display a wide variety of concerns and influences. Despite the differences, there are, nevertheless, many shared characteristics. The work shown in this book is all by young avant-garde firms. Also, their projects are located in very particular social, demographic, and geographical sectors of Los Angeles.

Patronage of the architectural avant-garde usually requires clients with certain levels of wealth and education. Patronage of overtly modernist houses, such as those featured here, has always accounted for only a small and specialized market in Los Angeles, albeit a far larger one than in virtually any other American city.

As David Gebhard has observed, the designs of the earlier avant-garde offices were never accepted by a wide public. Nor, like most of the firms in this book, did they generally receive large corporate or public commissions. Esther McCoy noted that before 1960 clients for modern houses in Southern California usually belonged to a certain culture of taste, singled out by their possession of real oil paintings, cut-leaf philodendrons, and leftist politics. But while changes in public taste limited the careers of pioneer modern-

ists like Irving Gill and the Green brothers, it would still be difficult to know just how well a modernist house would fare in a popularity contest with a Spanish colonial revival home.

But whatever the boundaries of popular taste, it is unquestionable that architects in Los Angeles are allowed far more freedom than in virtually any other region in the U.S. Even if the projects in this book had all the captions removed and all signs of context erased from the illustrations, it would still be obvious from the adventurousness of the projects that this is a book about architecture in Los Angeles. Avant-garde architects in Los Angeles use more unconventional forms, materials, and colors than those in other regions of the U.S. They do not always have communication with the public as a primary concern, and consequently they have the freedom to push the boundaries of what is possible in the creation of architecture as sculpture. In its broadest sense, then, much of the work in this book is modernist, abstract, and nonreferential to traditional building forms. The two local traditions that it most readily calls to mind are formal in nature.

These two fundamental trajectories in local architecture were identified by Henry-Russell Hitchcock in his seminal 1940 article "An Eastern Critic Looks at Western Architecture" in *California Arts and Architecture Magazine*. One is the high-art modernism of Gill, Wright, Schindler, and Neutra, and the other is the tradition of extravagance that goes as far back as the nineteenth-century work of the Newsom brothers and was later expressed in a series of wonderfully theatrical monuments, such as the Coca Cola Building in downtown Los Angeles, and the glorious tradition of strip and roadside architecture it represents.

Los Angeles is a place that can appear in many guises because of its varied geography, multiplicity of architectural styles, and complex overlay of mythic images, from Helen Hunt Jackson's imagined Hispanic past of the novel *Ramona* to the most elaborate myth-making machine of all, the entertainment industry. Michael Sorkin summed up this phenomenon with his concept of the Los Angelist, an observer of the city who makes urban connoisseurship a mode of existence. The Los Angelist "curates" his own personal vision of the city, and that vision becomes the city for him, whether it is Robert Winter writing about bungalows or the late John Beach pursuing pop architecture.

Those who have written most passionately and intelligently about the city's urbanism have pointed out the multiple layers of Los Angeles's sense of identity. Reyner Banham wrote about its urban design as a series of ecologies, treating them as a result of geographic, demographic, and lifestyle patterns. David Gebhard has addressed the city's need for fantasy and its conscious assumption of other times and places. Charles Moore has written about the ways in which identity could be chosen or manufactured in buildings such as the Mission Inn in Riverside. John Beach wrote about the energy, the openness, the sense of possibility that Los Angeles held during the boom years of the 1950s and 1960s. More recently, critic and historian Mike Davis has been reminding the architectural establishment how limited their view of the city has been, how many cultures and categories of places are left out of most definitions of what constitutes architectural importance in Los Angeles, and how easy it is to perceive much avant-garde architecture as hostile and antihumanistic.

In their writings, these critics were ever mindful of the dialectic between the city's mythic identities and its actual nature. But this dialectic is not always represented in the work found in this book. For example, one aspect of the Los Angeles tradition of experimentation has been the freedom to choose one's own identity to a greater degree than in many other American cities because of the acceptance of romantic fantasies and the willingness to identify with mythical identities. As Charles Moore wrote in *Los Angeles: The City Observed*, this is (or at least was) "... a place where romance repeatedly seduces reality, and only new arrivals cry 'Rape!'"

Southern California was fertile ground for theme buildings, such as the Santa Barbara County Courthouse and the Mission Inn, because of its reputation as a year-round resort where the vacation never ends. Los Angeles's most appealing buildings—from Graumann's Chinese Theater to the Hispanic courtyard apartment buildings of Zwebell—are the result of an artificially created identity, part of the well-established American belief that we are all free to reinvent ourselves. Such buildings resulted from the clever exploitation of a romanticized Southern California. In this idealized version of Southern California its own identity is melded with or contrasted with imagery from other times and places.

The work in this book is generally not concerned with rekindling a tradition of appropriation from other times and places, with the exception of some earlier local modernist traditions. When the architects shown here are concerned with other times, their choice for a period is the future, and it is a relatively gritty, mechanistic, and tough future they anticipate. The exquisitely rendered drawings of Neil Denari show urban constructions composed of machine-like forms. AKS Runo's models and drawings depict buildings as a series of abstract forms, without reference to human scale.

Earlier generations of Los Angeles architects often had, or claimed to have had, social interests related to their work, whether it was Richard Neutra's integration of indoor and outdoor space, Gregory Ain's interest in low-cost, mass-produced housing, or Raphael Soriano's belief in the virtues of steel construction. The present generation of avant-garde architects has generally not been as concerned with social issues as some earlier modernists, although there are obvious exceptions, such as Koning Eizenberg's low-income housing projects in Santa Monica.

My purpose here, however, is to explore just how regional the avant-garde work of Los Angeles is, and to what degree it reflects the local architectural traditions and urban context. Although many of the architects shown here were educated and trained (or come from) elsewhere, they have come to Los Angeles for freedom from history. They are seduced by the idea that Los Angeles promises unfettered self-expression, and hope to work in a city whose identity is not yet fully formed, so that they can help shape that identity.

The irony of this attitude, as Mike Davis has observed, is that Los Angeles is hardly the tabula rasa it is often credited to be. As the pace of technological change has increased, aspects of daily life pass into history with increasing speed. Many aspects of popular culture, such as the automobile, the single-family suburban home, and television, are twentieth-century phenomena and are all intimately associated with the history and development of Los Angeles. In this sense, Los Angeles is a giant, open-air museum of popular culture and the recent past.

Another irony is that Los Angeles now has its own architectural tradition of frequently iconoclastic reactions, so that making a one-of-a-kind gesture becomes part of a tradition of one-of-a-kind gestures. Janek Bielski's Desert House Project has unique qualities of its own, but it can be related to projects such as John Lautner's Bob Hope House in terms of being a sculptural form set off against the starkness of the desert landscape. Despite the fact that Los Angeles is often characterized as contextless, much of the work in this book has conscious or unconscious affinities with a specific Los Angeles vernacular, and with local high-art traditions. In fact, there are so many varying attitudes displayed that it would be almost impossible to design a structure that lacked a stylistic or typological precedent.

To the degree that there is local precedent for these projects, it is often either the commercial vernacular architecture or the vernacular urbanism of the region. The boldness of the commercial architecture is apparent in the work of Michele Saee, for instance, who took the name of the Ecru clothing store on Melrose Avenue and turned it into a brilliantly conceived metal abstraction that became the facade of the building. His project is a response to the surrounding cityscape, which is here transformed into a built reflection of a consumerist society, following the notion that the more a building needs to attract the public, the larger it should loom in the landscape.

To say a building is of the vernacular is to say that its builders did not have to give too much thought to the form or style in which it was built because they already knew such things. This is true when buildings are constructed by their users, as they often were in frontier America, but it is also true when they are constructed for profit by developers, such as the commercial vernacular of Los Angeles which also represents a commonly accepted way of doing things. By these criteria, the urban fabric of Los Angeles is a tissue of well-defined building types, including the commercial vernacular as well as the many permutations of multiple-unit housing, from the bungalow court of the 1910s to the stucco box apartment house of the 1950s and 1960s, and the upscale restaurants, single-family houses, and the recent incarnations of the stucco box apartment, as seen in Koning Eizenberg's housing projects.

Vernacular urban development also shapes the fabric of the city. Los Angeles is the result of 100 years of private property speculation focused on the primacy of the single-family house. While the larger context resulted from the distribution patterns of commercial building created by speculative development when a particular area was first opened up, any larger civic design or overriding plan, with the exception of planned communities such as Beverly Hills, has rarely occurred.

Because of this, a district with a strongly defined and regularized development pattern, such as Carthay Circle, appears as a discontinuous fragment within the larger urban structure. In general, while there are specific types of development which have a clearly recognizable internal order, such as walk streets in older foothill neighborhoods, it is the unity of the city as a whole that is hard to comprehend. Indeed, widely separated areas, such as the twin, canal-oriented seafront communities of Venice and Naples, often have more in common with each other due to similar development patterns than they have with immediate neighborhoods. While some projects in this book, such as those by Norman Millar, are clearly contextual in nature, many are not concerned with reinforcing the specific characteristics of their neighborhood.

One of the primary forces to shape Los Angeles has been, of course, the automobile. Since the 1920s much of the city's development has reflected the needs of the automobile as a primary determinant of urban form, which meant that most buildings increasingly needed large areas of parking. After World War II the practical and legal requirements for parking became so dramatic that landscaping was frequently desired, or required, in order to break up the vast stretches of asphalt. This has had the effect of isolating buildings from one another, giving them a relatively blank background so that the effect of other buildings, as context, is weakened.

In addition, the absence of a tightly knit urban fabric, and of neighborhoods made up of building types such as the row house that make up solidly and continuously built-up blocks, intensified a building's presence as a three-dimensional sculptural object. Consequently individual buildings in Los Angeles are not forced to acknowledge their immediate context as they might in a more traditional urban environment. Context, in the more suburban regions of Los Angeles, in fact, is often a matter of typology rather than propinquity: buildings are designed according to the rules of their building type, such as the hamburger stand or carwash, rather than their locations.

Given its innate multicentrism, one of the enduring debates about how Los Angeles should function as a city is the question of how much this multicentrism should be tampered with. Critics have objected to the physical isolation and lack of social interaction that the city's nonhierarchal development pattern produces, but they have also praised its concomitant atmosphere of freedom and independent thinking. There will always be a question of whether downtown Los Angeles really needs to play the same role as the downtown of Chicago or San Francisco. Perhaps in Los Angeles the flames of the backyard barbecue are always meant to burn brighter than those of any public gathering place. Some of the projects in this book, specifically Janek Bielski's Urban Mission and Johnson Favaro's town center for Huntington Beach, attempt to address such issues.

The city does not lack large-scale civic or public monuments. Witness the Los Angeles City Hall, Union Station, or the Griffith Park Observatory. However, those landmarks are not as important in creating a sense of place for local residents as comparable monuments in other cities might be. Los Angeles is not focused on Bertram Goodhue's Central Library in the same way that a landmark such as the Arc de Triomphe is an organizing point in Paris. Many of Los Angeles's true local landmarks are natural, such as the Santa Monica Mountains and the coastline. There are only a handful of monuments, such as the Hollywood sign, that function as reference points for the city as a whole. On the other hand, it is quite possible that the row of billboards on Sunset Strip plays a role for West Hollywood similar to that which the skyline of Manhattan does for New York. Hubert/Zelnio's proposed series of billboards is a wry commentary both on local air quality and the commercialized nature of the Los Angeles cityscape.

Responding to the various types of urban form in Los Angeles is one of the main issues that architects in this book have had to address. Confronted with the city's computer-circuit urbanism, complex building typologies and repertory of styles, they generally have had one of two reactions. One is to celebrate what is perceived as a lack of order as a liberating force. The other is to create a more clearly defined sense of place by adding large-scale formal elements, such as AKS Runo's Olympic West competition entry or the City Intervention project along the Harbor freeway in downtown Los Angeles by the Central Office of Architecture. C.O.A.'s projects are concerned with analyzing areas of the city and then playing up the qualities of continuity and discontinuity of a district's boundaries.

Another major influence on the architecture of Southern California is the effect of the benign climate, which does not require buildings to be engineered to withstand large amounts of snowfall or rainfall, humidity, violent hurricanes, or tornadoes. Also, because the need for insulation is lessened, buildings do not have to be meticulously constructed to seal out the weather. However, increasingly stringent earthquake regulations have limited the degree of insubstantiality that was previously possible. Architects are, therefore, less constrained by the limitations of construction materials than they might be elsewhere. Structures such as Josh Schweitzer's Monument, in which each room is housed in a separate building, would be unthinkable in a damper, colder climate. The Monument, however, is part of a long local tradition that includes the outdoor kitchens common in nineteenth-century adobes, the sleeping porches of the Greene brothers, or the exterior breezeways often found in garden and courtyard apartment complexes.

One of the most salient characteristics of modern architecture in Southern California has been the interplay between work that emphasizes volumetric building form and work that emphasizes the structural skeleton of the building. Some architects have worked largely within one category, such as Harwell Hamilton Harris, with skeletal buildings, or Irving Gill, with volumetric buildings, while others such as Lloyd Wright and Frank Gehry, have worked in both genres. Two other categories of design have been important in local architecture as well—those of neutrality/purity and expressionism. There is also a long tradition, noted by David Gebhard, of treating the building as a neutral box, often in stucco. The modularization and rationalization of structures and a minimalist approach to building form has also been a characteristic of Southern California architects. The most famous of these structures are the open steel-frame houses of the post–World War II Case Study houses program sponsored by John Entenza's *Arts and Architecture Magazine*, among them those by Pierre Koenig, Craig Ellwood, and Charles and Ray Eames. More recently, O'Herlihy + Warner has worked in this tradition in their Venice house addition project, while Charles and Elizabeth Lee's UCLA Childcare Center also reflects the continuing local interest in systems building.

Expressionism is a factor in the work of many local architects from the neo-orientalist craftsman designs of the Greene brothers to Meyer & Holler's Graumann's Chinese. Southern California architects built houses with jutting decks, balconies, and swooping eaves. Lloyd Wright designed houses with cavelike entrances, while John Lautner used the overturning Taliesin West fascia to help create the restless vocabulary of the 1950s coffee shop. It appears again in this volume in projects such as David Kellen's Fama restaurant. Southern California's high-art architecture is often loosely assembled from disparate parts, which could be seen as a reflection of the fragmented urban form of Los Angeles. To avantgarde architects in Los Angeles, both the blank surfaces of building walls and the frame of the building are seen as an opportunity to create abstract compositions of volumes and planes pieced together in constructivist compositions. Skeletal construction is used as a structurally expressive counterpoint to more conventional construction, and it is employed in much the same way the Russian constructivists employed tensile or skeletal elements.

Casual composition increases the sense of fragmentation and motion in the work. Such buildings suggest that they could just as easily have been put together in several other ways. They imply that they are the record of a process more than they are the embodiment of a final product. Schindler's Tischler and Janson houses fragmented space, and separated floor and roof plans long before the advent of the deconstruction. This tradition is seen here in buildings by Michele Saee, Josh Schweitzer, David Kellen, Lubowicki Lanier, and others.

The use of fragmented forms in so many of the projects may also reflect the architect's desire to avoid making completely comprehensible forms, reflecting the state of flux of a shifting and transitory society. Or it could simply be a preference for assembling buildings out of opposing materials. It could also be seen as architectural fashion, as a look, a style, or a fad. Finally, it also relates to developments in Southern Californian and American culture as well. In an era when jump cuts in music videos are *de rigueur* and surf trunks are made of vivid and clashing panels, it is not surprising that architecture is also designed as a set of contrasting parts.

In a project such as Lubowicki Lanier's Krane/Kellerman addition to Frank Gehry's earlier reworking of this house, each element reads as an attached piece of a larger whole. The Southern Californian acceptance of exposing ordinary materials, like concrete block, has given avant-garde architects the freedom to do the same, to use a material for what it really is, without apology, as a deliberate understatement through avoiding materials that are thought to be fancy or pretentious because they are deliberately pretty.

Some of this avant-garde work has certain qualities in common with commercial vernacular architecture. This vernacular also often has a fragmentary quality in which there is an acceptance of the semi-autonomous nature of individual building elements. Often, some elements are intended to be perceived as part of a finished design, while others are not. Thus, this architecture often has blank surfaces or dramatic oppositions between important and unimportant parts. One of its main characteristics is its lack of conventional architectonic unity. The relationship of the parts to the whole becomes unimportant; in fact, the parts are often conceived as complete events in their own right.

Ultimately, the work in this book deals as much or more with current architectural fashion, the training of the architects, and the kind of clients and commissions available to them, as it does with regional precedents. The most striking thing about the work is the vitality and the formidable level of talent displayed. What remains to be seen is if this interest in formal manipulation can be translated into the ability to address larger formal, civic, experiential and social concerns in the years to come.

Los Angeles's special conditions—the creation of a harmonious multiethnic community, the increasing bifurcation between rich and poor, the unique opportunities created by the weather, topography, and tolerance for experimentation, and problems of transportation and affordable housing—present social problems that stretch far beyond the purview of the architect. But for architects to ignore them in favor of empty form-making seems just as wrong as

assuming that they could be solely responsible for solving them. Nevertheless, one of the most intractable problems will remain the division between a hermetic avant-garde architectural culture and the public. A willingness to embody cultural norms shared by the public is often viewed, unfortunately, as a willingness to traffic with the twin devils of literal symbolism and the triumph of conformity over creativity.

**MICHELE SAEE**

Education:

Master of Arts in Architecture
University of Florence, 1981
Diploma in Urban Planning
Milan Polytechnic, 1982

Professional Experience:

Morphosis
Daniel Benjamin, Architect
SuperStudio
Zzigurat

# MICHELE SAEE

View from the dressing area

139

Entry

**Ecru Store 2** Marina del Rey, California 1989

Located in a suburban shopping mall, this design for a branch of Ecru, the high-fashion clothing store, uses many of the forms and materials of the original store on Melrose Avenue to create an expressive and open stage set for the mechandise.

Exterior       Bar

140

Plans and section

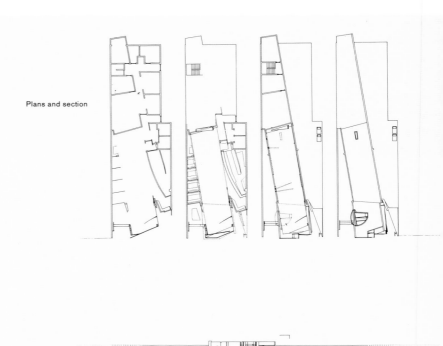

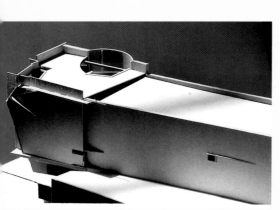

Model

**Japanese Restaurant**
Westwood Hills, California 1988

The main dining area of this
Japanese restaurant is a two-
story structure that rears its head

over the street below. Service
spaces fill much of the long,
narrow lot behind it.

Entrance door detail          Dining room

**Angeli Mare Restaurant**
Marina del Rey, California
1989-1990

Located immediately adjacent to Saee's Ecru Store, this restaurant is a branch of the Angeli Mare Restaurant for which he executed two previous designs. The restaurant's large dining hall is organized by a dynamic, wave-like ceiling structure, and the expansive dining area contrasts greatly with the constricted space of the bar.

141

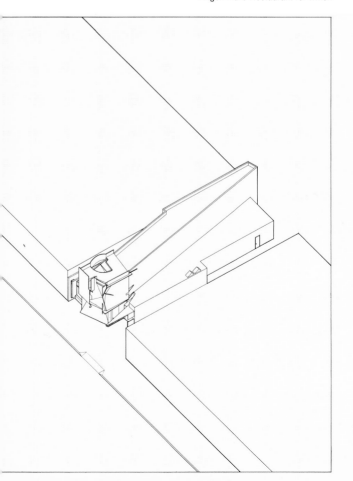

Axonometric

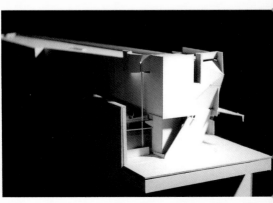

Model

Detail

**Design Express**
Los Angeles, California 1989

A 40,000-square-foot industrial building alongside a set of train tracks was converted into a showroom for high fashion furniture. The front of the building was designed as a facade facing a major boulevard. The only modulation of the cavernous space is created by a series of glass and steel vitrines. Welding and grinding marks and graffiti found on site were left intact. Together with the wood ceiling and concrete forms, these raw forms and the steel interventions contrast with the highly refined furniture on display.

143

View from street

Vitrines

**Ecru Store** Los Angeles, California 1988

Two existing stores were combined into a set of spaces for selling high fashion clothes and accessories. Ecru makes itself visible on Melrose Avenue through a series of steel plates that spell out its name. These plates take up the entire facade of the building, encompassing entrances and display windows. Inside, plywood panels, monumental steel tables and spider-like lamps animate the otherwise simple space.

Exterior detail

Entrance door detail

Exterior

Corner exterior

Clothes rack

Bar

Dining room

MICHELE SAEE

**Trattoria Angeli**

West Los Angeles, California

1987

A former carpet warehouse was gutted to accommodate a 3,000-square-foot Italian restaurant. The corner facade is at once mysterious, shielding the diners from the traffic of the busy boulevard, and from a billboard representing the forms of the inside. There, exposed bow-string trusses and a cantilevered bridge jut through a space that focusses on the kitchen, bar and entrance station. The materials are meant to be both rustic and elegant.

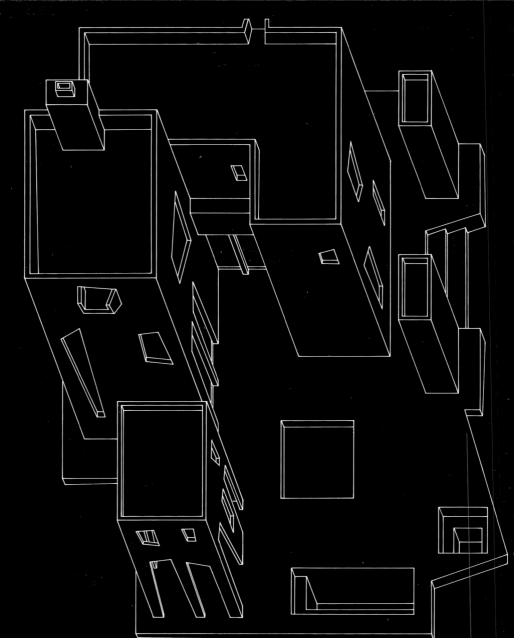

**JOSH DAWSON SCHWEITZER**

Education:

Bachelor of Arts
Pitzer College, Claremont, 1975
Master of Architecture
University of Kansas, 1980

Professional Experience:

Frank O. Gehry & Associates
Schweitzer-Kellen

146

# SCHWEITZER BIM

Plan

**The Monument** Joshua Tree, California 1987-1990

Exterior views

The Monument is an assemblage of one-room buildings, each containing a separate function. Its forms echo
the shapes of the large boulders that surround it.

**Hanauer Residence** Los Angeles, California  1990

The Hanauer Residence is the home and studio of a commercial photographer. To create a more intimate setting, the second-floor areas were designed as fragments of an urban landscape.

Models

**Tokunaga Residence** Los Angeles, California 1990-1991

The addition/renovation of the Tokunaga Residence has two principal elements: a second-story master
bedroom suite on top of an existing 1920s Spanish-style house, and a new detached garage studio. At the front
of the house, horizontal roof planes float over a new entry court providing a connection that unites the new
addition to the existing structure.

JOSH SCHWEITZER

150

**Border Grill 2** Santa Monica,
California  1990

Inspired by the tradition of mural
art in Central and South America,
an existing Mexican restaurant
interior was transformed through
a group of vibrantly colored

forms and textures. The
storefront becomes a gateway,
the murals become the
boundaries of an interior plaza,
and the floating ceiling becomes

a canopy of trees in which
goblins and spirits dance and
planets and stars shine.  The
paintings were created by the
British artists Huntley/Muir.

151

**Aloha Studio** Los Angeles,
California 1988

The former Aloha Swim School
now serves as the residence
for Josh Schweitzer and his
family. The site is dominated
by the huge swimming pool,
and circulation between the
structures is left open,
celebrating the mild Southern
California climate.

152

**L.A. Eyeworks** Costa Mesa, California 1988

L.A. Eyeworks is removed slightly from the pedestrian traffic in the South Coast Plaza Mall with a thin, veil-like wall of glass. The ceiling height varies dramatically, both dropping below and rising above the twelve-foot-high ceiling height of most mall shops.

153

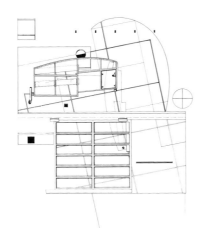

Window detail

**WARREN WAGNER**

Education:

Bachelor of Arts in Environmental Design
UC Santa Criz, 1981
Master of Architecture
UCLA Graduate School of Architecture
and Urban Planning, 1988

# WAGNER + WEBB

**WILLIAM WEBB**

Education:

Diploma in Environmental Design
Ontario College of Art, 1981
Bachelor of Architecture
Carleton University, 1987
Master of Architecture
UCLA Graduate School of Architecture
and Urban Planning, 1990

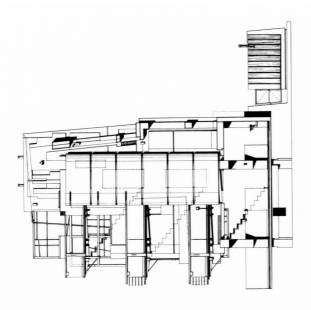

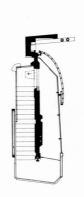

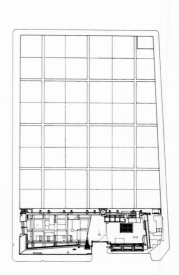

Site plan

## Lafaille Residence

Pacific Palisades, California
1988-1990

The transformation of this ranch-style home into what the owners call the "Mustang Ranch" is accomplished through the insertion of highly articulated and machined elements that open up and activate the spaces of the house.

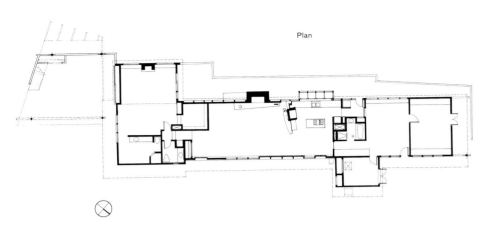

Plan

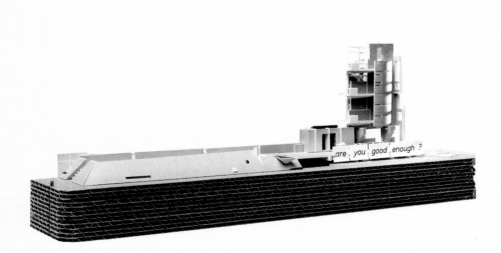

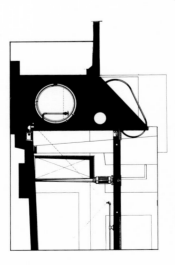

WAGNER + WEBB

Model

**Santa Monica Stone Garden Project**  Venice, California  1990

This small park is intended as a site for recycling and a place to collect and display scarce water. A tower with a view of the nearby ocean contrasts with the purposefully barren landscape of the plaza. The whole is meant as a "Los Angeles moment," representative of the nature of the urban desert.

**Long Woody House** Santa Fe,
New Mexico 1989-1990

This renovation of an adobe-
style house reflects the local
vernacular, provides an
appropriate setting for
the clients' collection of mission
furniture, and creates a series of
abstract spaces focused on the
changing light of the desert.

156

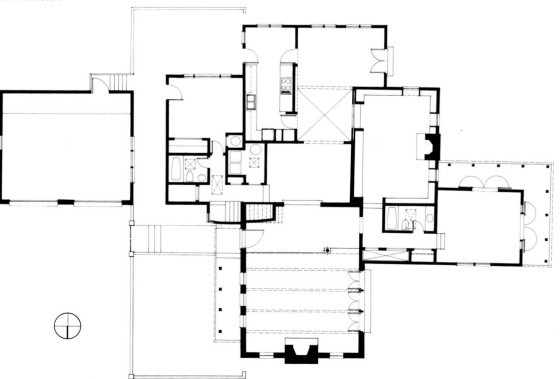

Plan

Porch

Living room

157

Front view

**Ridgerunner House** Venice, California 1991

The Ridgerunner House project consists of a second-floor addition placed on top of a an existing duplex.
The design treats some roofs as walls, some walls as fences, and some decks as roofs, creating a variegated
landscape screening views and domains of living without resorting to the creation of isolated boxes.

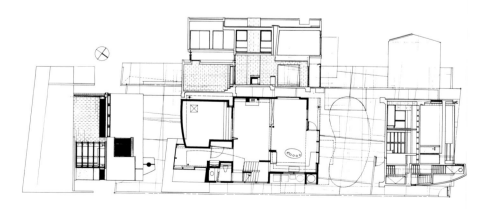

Plan/section/concept drawing

Model

**Shaw Residence** Marina del Rey, California 1989

The ground level of this house for a credit manager/wrestling promoter consists of open, loftlike spaces
constructed of masonry, concrete, and steel, all focusing on the swimming pool to the rear. The upper level is
built of conventional wood framing.